Life Lessons I Learned from My Dogs

A Woman's Story of Trauma, Healing, and the Power of Unconditional Love

Laurie Bowen, B.Ed., C.D.C., M.S.W.

 **LUCKY BOOK PUBLISHING**

Hardcover ISBN: 978-1-998287-40-6
Paperback ISBN: 978-1-998287-39-0
E-book ISBN: 978-1-998287-41-3
1st edition, November 2024.

"Dogs are not our whole life, but they make our lives whole. In their unconditional love, we find the strength to heal."

Roger Caras

My Gift To You

I am so grateful that you're here!

As my Gift to you, get FREE Access to the accompanying Audiobook by scanning the QR Code below or visiting
www.artsforlifeproductions.com

Dedication

For the dogs I have loved and lost, Queenie, Darkie, Kodi, Shamus, Babe, Chloe, and Simon. You helped me to heal. And to Lola, Lucy and Ethel, the newest loves of my life, I will forever be grateful to you.

My sincere appreciation and thanks goes to Dr. Andrew Thomas, of Brockville, Ontario, who is the first doctor to understand me.
A trauma-informed, empathetic doctor, who walked with me through the darkest times of my life and showed me my light. I will forever be grateful to him.

I dedicate this book to those who have survived childhood trauma and are now rising, just like me. You know who you are, witches.

All names, places and dates have been changed to protect the privacy of others.

Trigger Warning

This book contains sensitive content related to childhood abuse, including physical, emotional, psychological, and sexual abuse. The material presented may be distressing or triggering for some readers. Please proceed with caution and prioritize your mental and emotional well-being while reading. If you find the content overwhelming, consider taking breaks or seeking support from a trusted individual or mental health professional.

Because of You
The Words of The Victim
By Albert Dumont

You pushed me into raging waters
And I wonder
If my mind will ever heal

Because of you
I have forgotten the reasons
For the blossoms
And the purpose of the rain

Because of you
Instead of smiling into the dawn
I hide
And shed tear after tear

Because of you I feel as the rust
Which descends onto the beauty
Of our autumn's maple leaves

Because of you
Peace eludes me
And I see only heartache
Everywhere I turn

It is good now that you tell me
You are sorry
But tell me also
What you will do which will
Restore who and what I was
Before your cruelty
Pushed me into the raging waters

Because of Me
The Words of the
Perpetrator
By Albert Dumont

I pushed you into raging waters
And now I wonder
If you will ever be the same
Because of me
You have forgotten the reasons
For the blossoms
And the purpose of the rain

Because of me
Instead of smiling into the dawn
You hide
And shed tear after tear

Because of me
You feel as the rust
That descends onto the beauty
Of the autumn's maple leaves

Because of me
Peace eludes you
And you know only heartache
Everywhere you turn

I regret that I have caused you
Such great suffering
And I am sorry
What would you have me do
That would help you
Restore who and what you were
Before my cruelty
Pushed you into raging waters.

Table of Contents

Preface and Land Acknowledgement

Healing Minis Farm School is situated on unceded territories of the Algonquin and Anishinaabe Indigenous Peoples.

There are stories in this book that will trigger you, especially if you come from childhood trauma. The best thing to do when triggered is to meditate, in nature, preferably with an animal, like a dog. Deep breathing slows down our heart rates, and so does being with a horse. Learning to meditate is one of the most important things we can do in this lifetime, but many people believe that they can't meditate. I am here to say that you can.

I have a brain that has been labeled with Complex Post Traumatic Stress Disorder and

Attention Deficit Hyperactivity Disorder from Trauma, and I meditate daily, sometimes for hours. I also dissociate, which means to go to another place in your mind, kind of like dreaming, but you are still awake. It is a coping technique that many have learned to use to survive trauma. I have learned how to hypnotize myself and get myself into the calmest place that I can. I was diagnosed with fibromyalgia and PTSD in 1991 after a car accident. I continue to navigate the flare ups that come from stress.

I have tried just about every alternative therapy that there is, except micro-dosing mushrooms. Meditation in nature with animals is the optimal prescription to get through this life with less trauma. It's free. Don't get me wrong, counseling and psychotherapy are helpful, but not healing. Tapping on acupuncture points helps to calm us, but it doesn't heal us. Smelling lavender slows down our heart rate and helps to bring calm but it doesn't heal us. Neurofeedback will do the same. Trauma changes our brains, and our brains can heal, but it requires the opposite of what we want to do, we want to keep going, moving, being active. The last thing I want to do is slow down and be quiet, feel my emotions and listen to the divine within all of us, but this is exactly what I need. Feel it to heal it.

This book is my way of pointing you to the ways that I have found that bring true healing. It is why I opened Healing Minis Farm School. A place where people of all ages, races and genders, can find peace and healing, in nature, with animals. I am working to become a registered charity so that it can be free for everyone.

For those that have doubted me, talked negatively about me, or tried to stop me from achieving my goals, I thank you, because I am an alchemist and I turned your negativity into gold.

Laurie Bowen, B.Ed., C.D.C., M.S.W.

Author/Survivor

Introduction

When I was a little girl, I remember clearly thinking "One day, I am going to write a book and tell the whole world all about you." What I meant was, all about the abuse and neglect I experienced growing up with an abusive step-parent and my dead mother's molesting father, my grandfather. These difficult subjects are made lighter when told through the lessons learned from the dogs that have helped me transition through life's most difficult times. One day has arrived, and after decades of being both a patient and a practitioner of psychotherapy and counseling, I have learned that the healing can begin only when we learn to be quiet, and it is best done in nature with animals.

Why? Because animals don't judge, they only supply us with an immense amount of love and comfort. Horses and dogs are sentient beings, meaning that they experience emotions just like we do. They feel us. They follow their intuition, always. They teach us to do the same.

Dogs are here to teach us lessons because they truly want what is best for us. Their love is boundless. They love us without conditions and they never criticize us. They are always happy to see us and never ever give us the silent treatment. They come into our lives at just the right time, when we need them the most.

We can learn a lot from them. They have helped me heal from a lifetime of abuse. I feel safer with a dog than I do with a human, male or female. Dogs are dependable, lovable and loyal. They have a natural instinct to protect their humans. I know I wouldn't be the person I am today without their love and lessons, and I hope that you will be inspired by them too. This is a book about rising from the ashes and becoming an alchemist, a person who makes gold out of garbage.

Dogs are being used in courtrooms to comfort victims and are co-counsellors with many therapists, as we know the healing power that they possess. Taking a dog away from a grieving child is plain cruel, but it is what happened to me and my two sisters when our mother was tragically killed in a car accident with a train. I wasn't even two years old yet, and my mother and my dog were both gone. My dad was traumatized and returned to his studies shortly afterward, leaving me and my sisters alone to figure out our life without our trusting and loving mom or our dog a female lab, aptly named Queenie.

Chapter 1:
Queenie, Darkie and Grief

In the beginning, there was a dog named Queenie. I have no memory of this dog that my dad told me about. Queenie was with me when I was born up until the day my mom left this earth, just a month before my second birthday. She was a black lab, and my dad clearly adored her as his face lit up whenever he spoke of her. As a toddler, I remember thinking, "Then where is she, if she was ours?" She vanished with my mother, Alice, who was tragically killed at a railroad crossing near Huntsville, Ontario, where she is buried. It didn't take me long to realize the answer to this question. Queenie was, given away, and it was because of HER.

The woman he married only one and half years after my beloved mother left us because he said "She knew the Bible better than he did." Which was saying something, because he was studying to become an ordained minister, when she died in 1967. He was in Toronto during the week and at home with my mom and me and my two older sisters on the weekends. The only thing was, he was super busy on the weekends, preparing for the three sermons he had to give to three different churches. My mom was happy, I was told, staying home, taking care of her babies. At the time, we were one and a half, three and a half and five years young. I say that I was told because I have no memory of her. Even though she was my world for two short years, she was ripped away from us in an instant, and apparently, so was the dog. Another loss that would never truly heal. I have discovered that grief never ends, but it does get easier to carry.

My entire life, my grandparents and aunts and uncles lied to us about what took my mother away from us that tragic day. We were told that my grandmother had suffered a heart attack, but that was a lie. My grandfather told me the truth many years later, that it was because of him, that she left us with her friends to rush off after receiving a frantic call from her younger sister. He had been arrested after hitting Mrs. MacIntyre, my grandmother's best friend. My mother was rushing off to rescue him. The man who became my molester, forever changing the course of my life with his perversion. How ironic. Dogs never lie. Men and women, heck, toddlers even lie. Is there anyone who is willing to speak the truth? When I spoke up, I was called a liar.

There was always someone in need that took my dad, the preacher, away. Someone dying, someone crying, someone marrying and someone divorcing. He visited the broken, much like the man he preached about, but at home, it was a completely different story. At home, he let his new wife rule the roost and she was abusive. Verbally, emotionally and physically, while he sipped tea and ate date squares with the church ladies.

On Sunday morning I sat in the pew, hoping that I wouldn't have to sit beside her because if I moved or squirmed even a little bit, she would dig her nails into my tender skin. If I cried out, she did it harder. My dad was staring down from the pulpit while hundreds worshiped around me, and yet there I was, being abused, while my dad spoke about God and Jesus and the Holy Spirit, about family and about love. I was so confused.

I wished that we still had Queenie. Dogs show us love when the people in our lives can't or won't. I am still not completely sure which it is. I knew that I loved her and missed our dog, but we were sent to live with another minister's family after my mom died so that my dad could continue his studies. Queenie couldn't come with us. After a few months there, the wife started telling my dad that she thought we needed some grief counseling. In 1967, children didn't attend funerals, even if it was for their own mother. Who on Earth took care of us while they lowered our mother into an open grave? And where was our beloved dog Queenie who should have been there with us, helping us through the most horrific time of our young lives? She too was gone. My dad wasn't around either, and when he was, he was busy.

He soon moved us to another city to live with his sister, my beloved Auntie Em. She already had three teenagers, a husband, her mother and a dog to take care of, but she took us in for more than a year. In fact, on my dad's wedding day to my step-mother (a day I have never celebrated, nor ever will), she told him that he didn't have to do this, that she was happy taking care of us, and that's when he told her that this new wife knew more about the Bible than he did. She may have known and studied the bible, but she sure didn't live it. We lived with Aunt Em in a big house in the city where she and my dad were born and raised. Often, my older cousins would come by for supper, so there was always a houseful and another dog, named Darkie.

Now that I think about it, it was probably a racist name as my cousin, who brought him home after finding him on the street, was racist, as were many Irish people of the time. Darkie was my buddy and my friend, whom I spent countless hours petting. His favourite was behind his ears. Whenever the door would open, he would escape and my cousin would have to go looking for him. Darkie always came home though. He was always close by me, the youngest child of Alice.

Darkie was a mutt, and he was black with a little bit of white on his chest. I adored him, but the day I met my "new mother, she kicked him, and my life was never the same again. I was only three when I was told that I was going to be meeting my new mommy. Only thing is, I didn't hear "new", I heard "mommy," and I was so excited that after a year or more, Mommy was coming home. I remember sleeping with curlers in my hair and dressing in my best dress and shoes to meet her. My Auntie Em helped me to get ready. I couldn't understand why my sisters were sulking in the back stairwell, not wanting to meet her.

I ran to this woman and leapt onto her lap, only to be pushed away and witness her kicking Darkie. Who was this monster? This wasn't my mother. And why on Earth would she kick a sweet dog and push a three year old who had just lost her mother away? That was my first experience of rejection and abandonment that has followed me all of my days. This story was told to me by Auntie Em. I remember the curlers and the fancy dress and shoes, but I do not remember meeting the woman who would forever change the course of my life. In that instant, I decided that I wanted to be nothing like her.

Dogs are now being used as a source of comfort in court rooms and hospitals, hospices and jails. We have finally realized the healing power of dogs. Even though the wicked witch (as I still refer to her to this day), wouldn't allow us to have any pets, much less a dog, I waited for the day when I could have a dog of my own.

When I left my abusive husband in 2005 and fled to the other side of the province with my youngest child, the first thing that I did, was start looking for a dog at the local humane society and, I found him. A shepherd/collie mix who was six months old and who I named Shamus O'Rielly, because my ancestors hail from Ireland. I knew of another dog of the same name and breed from many years earlier. A dog I never forgot because his owner was abusive and beat the poor dog when it ate leftover dust in a bag of LSD.

That poor animal was thrown down the basement stairs after being beaten by my sister's crazed boyfriend, who later became her husband.

He screamed at me as I screamed at him. He ordered me not to go down to the basement and stormed off to bed. I went down to the basement and lay with Shamus all night long. From that day forward, I hated that man and vowed to rescue another Shamus and make things right again. Crazy idea, I know, but that is what I did when I found this amazing dog.

I waited and waited and waited and finally, his picture popped up on the Ottawa Humane Society's page. A six-month old shepherd/collie mix who was the spitting image of Shamus. I immediately went in and applied to adopt him. Upon leaving the Humane Society, I saw a man standing at a bus stop, a man who I hadn't seen in over 25 years, and it made a chill run down my spine. Standing right there before me as I drove by was the man who beat, raped and bit me violently, on several occasions.

I was stunned, and to this day, I do not know why the universe had me see him that day. Maybe it was to show me how far I have come from putting up with abusive men. I met him through my sister's boyfriend, as they all sold drugs and used us as mules. I was barely 18 and he was 26. I felt sorry for him and thought I could help him. I knew he was raised by an alcoholic father who beat him so had some level of compassion, and I made excuses for him too because it only happened when he was high or drunk, which was most of the time. It is coincidental how, all these years later, I made the same excuses for my now estranged husband, when he assaulted me after he drank too much at my sister's wedding in 2015.

I realize now that the Creator was showing me that this dog, Shamus, would keep me safe from men like him and the Creator is always right. Shamus would be my guide. If your dog doesn't like someone after getting to know them for a bit, the dog senses something that is incongruent in the person, meaning they aren't who they say they are. The way they are acting and the way they truly are is off balance. Dogs show us this. They are great for dating because, if your dog doesn't like your new boyfriend or girlfriend, they are right 100% of the time.

The most important thing in life is to be able to be quiet (meditate) and listen to your own inner voice, your own intuition. Dogs do this naturally. They will sit and listen for quite some time. They are ever present and aware of the now. They are our protectors, so if you feel scared a lot, get a guard dog. Everyone was afraid of Shamus, and that is how you want it to be.

Lola will growl and bark and be quite scary with everyone who comes here, but once she knows you, she will happily greet you. But there have been a few people with whom she will not settle. Now I pay attention and don't make excuses for people anymore. I give them time, of course, but if after several hours, the dog is still growling and nipping at them, well, something is wrong, and it's best to stay far, far, away from that person.

I ran to my Auntie Em to finally get rid of that abuser. By then, Darkie had been buried in the backyard of the new house they built on the river. Darkie was later joined by two miniature poodles, bulldozed over by the new owners when the house was sold after their passing. A brutal reminder that we all will return to dust.

Dogs are a constant comfort during the darkest of times. Every child should have the opportunity to have a dog in their life. So many are denied this simple treasure. Some people think that dogs are dirty and should not be allowed in the house, much less your bed. To them I say, people are much dirtier and vile than a dog will ever be.

The dog I have now is named Lola, and she is a highly sensitive dog who cuddles up with me in bed, even putting her head on my pillow while I hug her and bury my face into her neck. She snuggles with me when she knows that I am sad or lonely or not feeling well. She always comes at the right time, when I need her the most. I recently brought home two female puppies for Lola, and at first, she was less than pleased, growling at them, but it didn't take long before her mama instincts took over and she started to watch over them. It's a beautiful sight to behold. Lucy and Ethel, named aptly after the famous funny women from "The Lucille Ball Show" of the 50s and 60s are inseparable. Being red tick hound dogs with Bernese mix makes them not only adorable but extremely affectionate too!

I am so glad that 60 years later, dogs are being used to help victims speak their truth in courtrooms, to aid people to transition in peace and to bring healing to incarcerated men and women. Dog spelled backwards is God, and I don't think this is a coincidence. God loves us just like dogs do, it's religion that has taught us to hate.

Key Takeaway - The Lesson

If you are depressed, get a dog. And never ever take a dog away from a grieving child. That should be common sense. A dog will love you when the people in your life can't. They are the perfect antidepressant, forcing us to go out into nature even if all we want to do is stay in bed. Dogs are the perfect companions who love us unconditionally and will never betray us. They are also our protectors and help us to learn how to trust again. If you have experienced childhood trauma, they will help you to heal more than talking about it ever will.

When I left my first husband due to emotional and verbal abuse, the first thing I did was look for a dog like one I knew many years before named Shamus. I found him, and he made me feel safe and there is no better feeling in the world when you have grown up never feeling safe, secure or loved. Get a dog. You won't be sorry.

Chapter 2:
Shamus O'Rielly - Take No Shit

Shamus was a truly magnificent dog and a fierce protector. He growled at my neighbor when he came over to complain about the dog being in his yard. This man tried to hit Shamus with his black truck when trying to get his mail. I told him to go into his house so I could get the dog, but he just revved up his engine and moved back and forth trying to hit the dog as I screamed at him. He still lives across the street from me, and I am reminded of this vile man every day when I watch him leave in his black truck. Just the other day, he threatened to call the township because Lola went to his yard. She has never done that before.

I have no patience for assholes anymore.

Shamus knew, even before meeting him, that he had negative energy. Shamus was the best guard dog. Everyone who came to the door was terrified of him. Living as a single woman with a young daughter in the middle of nowhere, not knowing a soul, called for a guard dog, and that is exactly what Shamus was, our protector.

When he was a pup, he would run around the house all night, making sure that no intruder broke in. When he started wandering into the neighbor's yard, I had a doggie door built into the garage leading to a large kennel for him. But Shamus loved to run. I took him for walks every day, but he needed to run, and this was before dog parks. Whenever he happened to get loose, he ran and ran and ran and ran and rarely left the property. When he was tired out, he would come in. There was no catching him, and he wouldn't come for treats. He would come when he was good and ready. And he never wanted to be in the house either. He was so much happier outside.

I got him in June 2005 only a few months after I had moved from one end of Ontario to the other to get away from my abusive husband and my first divorce. It was the happiest day of my life, the day I drove the moving truck down the 401 Highway to freedom. I met my second husband six months after I moved, and the first time he came to my house, Shamus got loose and he tried to catch him (which he did), and then he restrained the dog with his hand around Shamus' neck and body. Well, Shamus bit him multiple times on his hand. I couldn't believe that my dog had bitten my new boyfriend. This was a sign, a red flag, they call it, and there were many that I chose to ignore. I don't ignore them anymore. Now I see them everywhere. Being single at 60 isn't so bad. In fact, I rather like it.

At the time, Artie took responsibility for restraining him so I was okay about it. Artie never took responsibility for anything beyond that day. Ever. He blamed me if it rained that day. His thinking was so negative that it was draining day after day after miserable day. As he aged, he only got worse until dementia started taking over in his late 50s and early 60s. I haven't seen or spoken to him in over 9 months, the longest we have ever gone with no contact. I have to say, it has been exhilarating not to be under the suffocating judgment of a perfectionist, workaholic and narcissist. Pay attention to who your dog loves, and most importantly, who your dog hates.

If a dog doesn't like a person and never warms up to them, be very wary of that person. I ended up marrying him, and it was a hell of my own making. The beginning of this relationship was great because he traveled for work and was gone for three weeks and home for three weeks. When he was home, his daughters and sisters and friends all wanted to see him, of course, so they were very busy times. Even though I complained when he was gone, I actually enjoyed my time alone. I was the one who saw the ad in the newspaper for a professor of trades job at a prestigious college and sent his resume and cover letter in. He, of course, got the interview and the job and retired from an excellent career that paid him handsomely. But, if you ask him, I spent all of his money and brought him to ruin. Perspective is everything.

I still have a piece of my kitchen floor that Shamus chewed as a pup along with the corners of my piano bench. He was an only dog for about a year when my husband moved his dog Kodi in with us. Kodi was probably already 15 years old and built like a brick wall. She was stout and all muscle and resembled the Kodiak Bear, which is how she got her name. I fell in love with her the minute I met her and begged my new boyfriend to let me take care of her while he was away.

She was chained up at his father's house, and the other neighbors' dogs would come around and eat her food. She had a food issue until the very end. There was more than one occasion when I had to stop her from nipping at Shamus for being near her food bowl. She always had everything that she wanted, but being left without, well, it changes you.

I should know because the day my mother left this world was the day everything changed for the worse. Everyone around me was sad. Everyone. Not a happy face in sight. All of the sudden the darkest of dark clouds came over my life and stayed for most of it. I was told that my mother was an angel in heaven. I didn't understand why she had to go. I didn't understand why my dad was rarely around or why my sisters were like zombies. And our dog, Queenie, was gone.

I understand feeling left out, abandoned, rejected and alone. It had always been the dogs in my life who taught me about love when the people were unable or unwilling to. I have always loved dogs, so very much, and now, I know why. They literally saved my life. Babies will die if they don't get physical touch and love. I grew up learning how to love from the dogs who just happened to be in my life at the exact time that I needed them.

My step-mother, who I always refer to as "the wicked witch", threw a sweet little puppy down cement steps when it followed me home from the library one day. I am traumatized by it, to this day, because we all know that I wanted the puppy to follow me home. I was the one who brought it to the wicked witch, not thinking that she would do such a horrible thing to an innocent puppy but, at the tender age of three or four I should have known better. From the moment we take our first breath, we start to sense and pick up the energy from our parents or caregivers, and we either become just like them or, the complete opposite. I have worked very hard to become the latter.

Shamus was my way of rectifying a horrible situation that happened in the past. If I could love another Shamus, then I could make up for the abusive behavior of one man, the father of my niece and nephews. He is gone now from this earth, and I believe he realizes the great harm he caused so many people with his alcohol and drug issues and his own childhood trauma that has been passed down from generation to generation until someone, usually the "black sheep" stops it at their door.

He was abused by his father and uncle, and he abused his siblings and children and wife and some of them (although not all), have become abusers too, so the cycle of abuse continues to this day. It stops here, at my door. There won't be any more abusive people allowed into my sanctuary. I will always have a loyal dog like Shamus to protect me, and now their names are

Lola, Ethel and Lucy. When people let you down, dogs are there to show us what true love is.

True love doesn't leave. True love knows how to just sit with you in the midst of your storm and help you to ride it out until you reach the other side, where the waters are calm and you can find peace. Dogs are the best antidepressant in the world. They get you out of the house and walking several times a day. They crave our affection and freely give it back to us. They are extremely happy when we come back home. No one in my life has ever been as wonderful to me as dogs have. No one has loved me like my dogs have. I honestly don't think that I would be here today if I hadn't had these amazing creatures in my life.

Shamus died young at the age of nine, and I think he either got into something, was poisoned or affected by shots and a tranquilizer given to him by the vet two weeks earlier. I came home at 7 pm from work on a Friday and Shamus had been vomiting. He was in the house, in the basement. He never came in the house, so I knew he was sick. He was with my daughter and slept outside of her bedroom.

In retrospect, I wish I would have called the emergency vet then and there but truth be told I was afraid of my then husband's reaction to the bill. He is a very, very, very, cheap person, more than frugal, and he was controlling me with his moods. I decided I would call the vet first thing in the morning. I got up at 6 am and went to check on Shamus, and he was dead. He was gone. My beautiful protector had left me, and my heart was so full of guilt and grief. I had let him down.

I had to call someone to help me bury him, and he is buried alongside Kodi, who went before him. I also regret not having an autopsy done to determine exactly what caused this healthy dog to die overnight. Again, I was afraid of my husband's reaction to the bill. He wasn't home that day and didn't answer my calls, so I was alone, to deal with it.

I felt so guilty, like I had let this poor dog down and that I was an awful dog owner. I know that I did the best that I could with what I had, but many years later my husband told me that "we started having issues in our marriage when you decided to grow a set of balls". I guess that means stand up for yourself. That's what Shamus taught me, to stand up for myself and to follow my instincts, no matter where they may take me.

When you know better, you can do better, and I know better now than to let another person control my decisions and ultimately my life. Narcissists are highly attracted to empaths as they share a trauma bond. The empath seeks to heal their narcissistic partner, while the narcissist seeks to control. It is an insidious dance that will never be beautiful.

When I moved in 2005 across the province, I started listening to my own intuition and allowed myself to hear from heaven. The "church" teaches us not to talk to soothsayers and psychics nor pay attention to the stars in order to keep us from the truth which is that we can all speak to our loved ones that have passed. We just have to be quiet and practice.

I was so bothered by it that I went to see an elderly pastor for over a year to try to see if this was true. That dead people really can talk to us. This pastor said that he believed that because of my life's circumstances, God has indeed allowed me to have a telephone line to heaven, but if I ever tell anyone he said that, he will deny it. It was like he gave me permission to continue what I already started which was talking to the angels that have been trying to talk to me my whole life, and in particular, my mother, Alice. I always know it is her when she calls me "baby girl." Another dear friend, Terry, calls me Laur. I know who they are and they are always around me. They work with the animals to help me feel loved in a world that is so lacking in it.

There is a prayer called the Hawaiian Prayer that I have said to Artie hundreds of times, and it never really penetrated his heart, but it helps me to forgive and move in love instead of in fear.

It is simply: "I love you. I am so sorry. Please forgive me. Thank-you."

Say it to yourself, say it to the people you love, just say it. It helps to remove the negative feelings that empaths pick up so easily. Dogs are empaths. Horses are empaths. Survivors of childhood abuse can be empaths, and they can also be narcissists, and they are often attracted to one another. I realize now that Artie and I had a trauma bond. Although I loved him deeply, he was not capable of such love, although parts of him craved it.

His life became a tug of war and it unfortunately ended, in war. Divorce is a kind of war, especially if the other person is deranged and threatening to "shoot you in the fucking head", and even worse is when you believe them. Finding the evidence only further nails the coffin shut on this thing called marriage. Getting out of it without losing everything you have spent your lifetime building is daunting for the strongest of us. Thank God I have my sister, helping me to wade through the legal system so that justice can finally come into my life.

He is trying to take my home, my little farm, my soon to be non-profit, Healing Minis Farm School, that I bought by myself, 19 years ago and make me a homeless woman with three miniature horses and three dogs. The lover in me has gone to sleep and the warrior has awakened. That's all I can say about that. I have learned that having a fence around your property is more about safety than it is about keeping people out or being rude.

It is putting up a boundary, saying that you cannot come here without my permission.

If you own your own home and you get married, make sure you have your new partner sign a prenuptial agreement. Never in a million years would I have guessed the outcome of my second marriage to be so dramatic and vile. Mental illness, like dementia can lead to violence if left untreated. I worked in a jail for people like that and now find myself married to one, and yet the system isn't seeing it or else why would they let him plead not guilty? I pray that someone opens their eyes, but I have done all that I can and now I just need to speak the truth. And the truth is the truth, no matter how you slice it.

Artie, unfortunately, decided to plead not guilty, and now there is going to be a trial in a few months time and I have already been subpoenaed to testify. It is my deepest hope that I won't have to. When I don't know what else to do, I say to myself, I love you, I am so sorry, please forgive me, thank-you.

Key Takeaway - The Lesson

Learn to stand up for yourself. When you begin to, people won't like it, but do it anyway. There is no need to yell. A quiet, calm assertion is all that you need. Learn to meditate so that you can connect with your inner guides and strengthen your intuition. And always, trust yourself. No one has your back better than you do. Well, no one but your dog. They always have our backs. My second husband came with a dog who taught me patience and to never give up. She was very elderly when she arrived in my life, and I was honored to walk her into her transition. I know that she is lying under a big tree, waiting for me, and will be running to greet me when my time comes.

Chapter 3:
Kodi - Steady As She Goes

Kodi had such a gentle spirit, but she scared me the first time I witnessed her nip and growl at Shamus because he came too close to her bowl. It really shocked me because I had never seen that side of her. She showed me that even at her old age, she could still defend me.

I would take her with me as I walked Shamus and she would be lagging behind. Shamus would be pulling on the lead to get going and Kodi would be sauntering down the road, no worry in the world. She would walk down the middle of the road without a care, and when she was tired, she would simply lie down and there was no moving her.

Many times, I tried to get her out of my flower garden where she had dug a hole to lie down in. Time after time, she returned to the same spot and just looked at me with those deep brown eyes of hers that said, "Oh come on, let me stay here. I just dug this hole and it's nice and comfy and, most of all, cool." I always gave in. I knew she wouldn't be with me for much longer as she was very elderly, and I can always grow flowers somewhere else.

Kodi would often lie under a beautiful evergreen tree here at Healing Minis Farm School, and it has become a resting spot for many who come to this farm to find peace and learn how to rest. Shortly after she passed away, the tree fell over in a fierce wind and snow storm, and in the spring, it was on its side and still growing! It is the funniest tree I have ever seen as it continues to grow lying down. Kodi laid here and she taught me to wait. And wait. And wait some more. And do it with a smile on my face too. She led me to the now, and I didn't even realize it until just now. Her spirit lives on in me.

Whenever I came home, she would get up and slowly make her way to me. Gone were the days of running and jumping, it would take her several minutes just to make her way over to the car. I would stand there and wait for her because she waited for me the whole day. I would rub her belly as she stared up at me with her loving eyes. She too never wanted to come in the house. Her fur made her hot so she preferred to be outdoors and could be found covered in snow in the middle of a snow storm with just her black, brown and white nose sticking out. She must have had some Bernese Mountain Dog in her, maybe mixed with a malamute, because she was solid as a rock.

Kodi never had to be on a leash or kept in a kennel because she never wandered off the property. She was free to roam on six acres of wetlands that backs onto the South Nation River. I was so happy that she was never chained up again and spent her final years free.

She was the first dog to be buried in the Forget Me Not garden on my property. Fitting, I think, for my life and for hers. She will never be forgotten as she taught me to be patient and to learn how to wait, for it is in waiting when the seed takes root and sprouts above the dark earth to grow into the beautiful flower it has always been. The forget me not flower reminds us that everything takes time.

In order to have a flower, you must first plant a seed, then you must water it and care for it, making sure that it has the proper amount of light in order to grow. Without these ingredients, it will die. Have you ever planted seeds and then forgotten to water them? They don't grow. They need water, and when they sprout, they need light. Without it, they won't grow. We are the same way. Water and light represent love. Without it, we don't grow. When the adults around us are clueless as to what real love is, the child has to find it somewhere else and it often comes from dogs and animals in general. That's where I found it. Water is indeed life, and we have water protectors now who are Indigenous warriors fighting to keep our water systems clean, but it is an uphill battle. There is a reserve in Ontario that hasn't had clean water for more than 30 years. That is disgraceful and unbelievable for a country as rich as Canada.

Many times, it is the small things that do make the biggest impact, like water, for example. Plants need it, animals need it and we need it, yet we have polluted it to the point that it is now causing all of us unnecessary harm in the form of climate change. The future generation is standing up to the status quo. Look at the young girl from Sweden, Greta Thunburg, who has taken the political leaders to task over climate change, or our own Autumn Peltier, an Indigenous Water Protector who is holding Canada responsible for making sure everyone has clean water.

Recently, universities across Canada have been protesting the war in Palestine and the Genocide that we are witnessing there and in The Dominic Republic of Congo. The young people are leading the way. Love is the way and they know it. Hate, division, religion and war are not what the youth of today are looking for. They want the simple things in life, like, clean water, affordable housing, a living wage and a healthy planet. Our dogs show us how a simple belly rub can change your mood. A walk with your dog can improve not only your physical health, but your mental health as well.

Because dogs are always in the now, they are never worried about the future or depressed about the past. They teach us how to be present, which is where the divine is found. They teach us how to love by showing us their love for us. You are never truly alone when you have a dog.

Kodi had such a thick mane around her neck that she always reminded me of a sunflower. She was bright and brilliant like a sunflower too, and I plant them on her grave. This has become a sacred place where I stop and meditate, sending my love to her, wherever she may be. My grandson calls it "Grandma's quiet spot". I know that dogs never really leave us, even if we can't see them anymore. They are always close by, reminding us how to love. Even in the darkest hours, love survives.

Key Takeaway - The Lesson

Learn to wait. Learn to enjoy waiting. Learn to embrace the NOW. Kodi taught me to wait. And to do it with a grateful heart too. She also taught me to never give up. Rest, if you must, but make sure that you always rise again the next day and do the very best that you can to make it through. Kodi, although she was old and probably had arthritis, kept going until it was time for her to finally rest.

The sun will come out again and you will find joy again. Weeping may endure for a night, but joy comes in the morning. We cannot have joy without sorrow, light without darkness or life without death. It is all so paradoxical. After losing a beloved pet, another one will come along for you to love and nourish again. Herding dogs are the best for a farm, and my little farm needs them. www.healingminisfarmschool.com is a place where you can find peace and healing and where these beloved dogs are buried in the Forget Me Not Garden.

Chapter 4:
Babe - My Soulmate

For ten years, I worked as a Social Worker for the Community Care Access Center in my local community. This job was amazing, as I got to travel all over the place, visiting people in their homes, much like my own father did as a minister, except I was helping people to connect to the resources in their community or provide some supportive counseling. I arrived at a house, near the end of the dirt road, that had a very long driveway. As I approached the big white, farm house, I saw a yard littered with old vehicles and trailers,and someone was living in one. I told him I was looking for Joe, and he motioned for me to go up to the house further down the driveway.

I could hear a dog barking as I drove further and parked under a big tree. There was a, huge white dog, barking at me. She was chained up and couldn't quite reach me. As I approached, I spoke to her in a calm voice and came close enough for her to sniff me. I saw that her tail was wagging, and we quickly became fast friends. Her name was Babe, and she was a great white Pyrenees dog who had been abandoned by her owner when she went into a rehabilitation center. My client, Joe, had cancer and was having a hard time taking care of himself, let alone a dog. He already had a little dog of his own.

Joe was a lively fellow who loved to laugh, and laugh we did. He took quite a liking to me and said that he wanted to adopt me as his daughter. I just laughed off his jokes. We would have a cup of tea and he would tell me about the latest health issue he was facing. He played guitar and could always be heard laughing. That is what I remember most about him, his great, big, gregarious laugh. I met with him every week for many months, but as it goes with government funded services, the day came when he was discharged from my case load. Joe would have nothing of the sort. He would call me and leave lovely voice mail messages asking me to come and visit and have a cup of tea with him and bring my husband and so I did. I know we weren't suppose to be friends with our clients, but I waited the required year and then visited him. Rules were made to be broken. Always follow your heart.

His health had declined and the cancer had spread, and he could no longer take care of Babe. He said, "You should take her." And so I did. I took that great, big, white, fluffy dog home with me, and she lived out the rest of her days in paradise. Babe loved to wander and often got loose at Joe's place with the little dog, but they always made their way home. Well, Babe arrived after Kodi had died and before Simon (the stray beagle) showed up, so her timing was perfect. Shamus needed a friend, but it was short lived as he passed away suddenly, only a few months later.

Babe would wander, so I always walked her on a leash. It took her a while to get used to being walked on a leash as she had never been walked before. I noticed that she was limping so started using a strap to help support her rear legs.

Babe was my soulmate. She comforted me through some of the most difficult moments of my life. My three-year-old grandson, who rarely hugged anyone, would be found lying on Babe's back with his little arms around her neck, a huge grin on his face. I knew that this dog was special. She was only with me a few years, as her hips began to wear, and the dreadful day came when I had to call the vet because she could no longer walk. The vet had told me that I should consider putting her down the year prior and I argued with her. I started giving Babe a drop of Rick Simpson oil, long before legalization, and she was without pain for more than a year. We went on many adventures together those first few months, and then along came Simon. I will never forget the day.

It was a hot summer day, and my three-year-old granddaughter was visiting and came running inside to tell me that there was a dog in the front yard. There was Simon. A beagle who had heartworm disease. He was terrified of people. I got some water and food and left them out for him. He wouldn't come near me, but for my granddaughter, he did. He quickly realized that we are loving people and my daughter fell in love with him. She got a summer job and used all of her paycheck to pay for the medicine that Simon needed. That is true love.

I can't write a chapter about Babe without writing about Simon because, as soon as they met, they were inseparable. They ran off together within the first few days of meeting, and Simon knew where home was after spending a night alone outside a few miles from home. I was able to pick up Babe after I posted on social media. She was more trusting of people and went into a lady's car but Simon was running wild. I had to go home without him. The next day he showed up at home and he never left the property again.

I would take Babe for walks on the leash while Simon ran circles around us. Sometimes he would dash in front of me and startle me. After he left this earth, I continued to sense his youthful spirit dashing around me and sometimes, I catch a glimpse of his shadow. He has never left me, even though the day he did was one of the most devastating. But this chapter is about Babe, not Simon. Like I said, they were inseparable.

They slept together on the same pillow, followed each other around, played with each other, ate beside one another were the epitome of best friends. Babe was so very loyal to this little dog that showed up sick and afraid, especially of men. My husband, at one point, threatened divorce because for a few months, we had three dogs. Shamus died shortly after Simon arrived. Simon was with Shamus when he started vomiting, as was Babe. They would be in the garage where it was cooler in the summer with a doggie door to a huge 14-foot high kennel because Shamus could jump really high.

As dogs do, Simon made his mark everywhere, destroying a wall in the basement and he also loved to dig holes, which infuriated my husband. Simon was terrified of him and rightly so. I figured that Simon was probably kept with other beagles as hunting dogs, and when he got sick, the hunter just let him go. He was three when he showed up at our door. His silky ears and deep, dark brown eyes just drew me in. My daughter refused to allow me to take him to the humane society and ultimately won the fight. I would hear about the holes he created until the regrettable day that he died. Shamus died only a few months after both Babe and Simon arrived, so the trio became a duo, and what a duo they were.

Babe was much older than Simon so didn't care for the energy, but she dutifully put up with it. Babe spent most of her time with Simon, and since my daughter had adopted him, they both were in her room until it was time to eat. Those two were spoiled, as I started to cook for Babe since she was elderly and needed a little extra, and Simon didn't mind in the least. They taught me about friendship and how true, devoted friendship is such a beautiful gift.

I hope that you find a friend like Babe. A friend, who knows how to just sit with you when you need a shoulder to cry on. A friend who will defend you no matter what. A friend, who wants to spend time with you. A friend who never leaves you.

Babe deteriorated to the point where she could no longer walk and was put down in the front yard while her head lay in my lap. I loved her so deeply and knew that Joe was on the other side, having succumbed to cancer, waiting for her. I told him "I think you should take her now Joe. I will be along in due time, but for now, you can have your friend back. Until we meet again." And with that my soulmate was gone. Simon was so sad without her, but another Pyrenees came along a few weeks later, who was named Chloe. It seems they always come at just the right time if you are open to it.

It has taken me many, many, many, years to figure out what a true friend is. I have a few now and I cherish them greatly. We can look to dogs to see what a true friend is. People who are empaths have to be particularly careful of who they allow into their inner sanctum. I know that now, after I learned it the hard way of course. Protect your own home and heart above all else because in the end, you are all that you really have. Animals will never let you down.

My horses knew when I was having a heart attack, and the three of them surrounded me in a circle. I had pain in my chest and bent over slightly, holding my chest while I breathed through the pain. Emmie put her forehead on mine, and I went to the most beautiful and tranquil place where I heard a voice say to me, "You are having a heart attack, but you are going to be fine." There was an immense amount of peace, like ok, lets get on with it then. I went to a walk-in clinic and the female physician ordered me to the nearest ER, where I was then put in an ambulance to go to the Heart Institute Critical Care Unit where they inserted five stents. My main artery was 100% blocked and the other four were 80% blocked. The surgeon told me that the Pfizer vaccine actually saved my life as it triggered the heart attack. I had been having them for a week, thinking it was the flu or a fibro flare up, never considering heart disease that both my father and maternal grandmother had. Artie dropped me off at the nearest hospital, and I didn't see him again until his birthday in June. We were both scared, and it changed our perspective, as near death often does.

The person who you love the most can become the person who ends up trying to bury you, literally. It is very hard to trust someone completely especially when you have lived a lifetime with people who continually break your trust. In dogs, you can trust. A dog will never betray you or cause you harm. A dog truly does want the best for you. If you are feeling down, it's your dog that will climb into your lap and rest their head upon your chest and give you the warmth and love that you need to feel better. People can be the same but they rarely are. Dogs be there for you, without fail, every single time that you need them to be, and that is true love. If you can't find a friend like that, then go adopt a dog.

Key Takeaway - The Lesson

Pay attention to the opportunities for love that you turn down. My husband was okay with having Babe because Shamus needed a buddy, but it turned out, Shamus died a few months after Babe arrived. Simon arrived only a month before Shamus died. We had three dogs for one month and my husband wasn't happy. At one point he said "me or the dog". He isn't here anymore, but the dog is buried in the garden with the others.

Love comes in unexpected ways and places. Had I ignored Joe's voice mail messages, and played by "the rules", I would have missed out on walking with Babe as well as Joe, through their transitions between earth and the beyond, which is the most sacred time. Pay attention to the signs for love because they are always around us. We are too busy to notice them, but they are there. For me they are butterflies and cardinals, repeating numbers and feathers, sometimes a soft voice that tells me what is about to happen. We all have this inner guidance at our disposal, but we have to be quiet to hear it.

Learn to meditate. Meditate with your dog in nature. It's amazing. Dogs are always ready for an adventure, and you should be too. Most of all, learn to live outside the box. Don't follow what everyone else is doing; create your own path. Find like minded people. You don't need a dozen, one or two loyal and loving friends will do, and don't limit yourself to race or age. I prefer to spend my time with the youth of the world because they are the ones who are going are leading the way to peace. The universe is always conspiring for your good, all the time. Don't ever be afraid to go outside the lines. Fear is what stops us from experiencing the creator's richest blessings. Human existence is about love, but so many people don't even know what it is. You need only to look to a dog to discover what true love really looks like.

_____

Chapter 5:
Chloe – Don't Be Afraid to Go Outside the Lines

Babe had barely been gone a week when my daughter and her then boyfriend came to me, asking if they could adopt their friend's mother's dog. The mother was selling her house and moving to an apartment and wouldn't have room for a Pyrenees. Yes, another Pyrenees on the heels of losing Babe. These two teens begged me to take her in, and so I did.

Chloe was full of fleas and her skin was scabbed from her scratching so much. She had an ear infection and would pee huge puddles on my hardwood floor, staining it black forevermore. I took her out every few hours but she would still pee in the living room, in the same place, every day. I couldn't understand it, so I took her to the vet. They discovered that she had a tumor on her pituitary gland that was causing her to be really thirsty with thus the constant need to urinate. She also had Cushing's disease.

She too received home cooked meals as I navigated her illness. The vet said she would be lucky to survive another year. It was then that I decided to give her cannabis oil, one drop a day, and for the next two years she was fantastic. She played with Simon but was never as close with him as Babe had been. She managed to surpass Simon, only by a few months though. By September 2018, they were all gone including my dad who passed away September 3, 2018, and upon returning from the funeral, our cat, Molly, went missing, never to be found again. So much loss in such a short time is overwhelming. Although I desperately wanted and needed another dog, I waited for over three years before Lola found me.

Chloe lived longer because of cannabis and that is thinking outside the box. Cannabis wasn't even legal yet, but I had a license to grow and consume it as I have fibromyalgia, complex post-traumatic stress disorder and ADHD, all linked to childhood trauma. I was diagnosed with fibromyalgia and PTSD over 30 years ago when we had barely even heard of them. A woman where I worked had it and couldn't get off of her couch. I determined that was not going to happen to me so I simply forgot about it and navigated the chronic pain and fatigue, brain fog and depression the best that I could and still do.. Throughout my journey of recovery, I have found that hypnotherapy and acupuncture coupled with meditation with horses in nature have kept me balanced. I take natural supplements and a new medication for ADHD that is life changing. It was like a light switch was switched on and I could finally see and get things done. Gone were the scattered thoughts, feeling like a hamster on a wheel working hard but never really getting anywhere, or so I thought. I have, finally, found my peace. And my soon-to-be ex-husband wants to take it from me.

Chloe also spent a lot of time in my daughter's room but was always close by for meals and walks. She came to me with many health issues, and I helped her to resolve them. Chloe taught me that it's important not to go along with what everyone else is saying and to do your own research and due diligence. At the time, cannabis wasn't legal unless you had a doctor's approval, and finding a doctor who even knew anything about cannabis was more than challenging. It just wasn't available. And giving it to dogs unheard of. I have always been ahead of my time.

During this time I found a psychologist close by who treated PTSD with cannabis and felt that it was the best thing for this disorder. I saw him five times, and he gave me the trilogy audiobook called "Conversations With God." That book awakened me to the truth about religion and the Bible that I had been hearing about for many years. Quite frankly, we can't trust any religious texts because they have all been changed to suit the needs and desires of the men who were in power at the time. A loving god would never send their child into a pit of fire, nor would he/she require the shedding of blood for our so called sins. Now that I am out of it, I can't believe how long I held on to these beliefs. I am so glad that I am finally free.

I had been using cannabis for many years after moving here in 2005, as my new doctor would not continue to prescribe the narcotics I was given in Windsor. I rarely used them and only got a script once per year, but she still would not prescribe any narcotics and instead tried me on all kinds of different meds, all of them making me feel anxious. Now I realize that I was misdiagnosed, and what she gave me could never have helped. She didn't take the time to investigate, instead, I started using cannabis and discovered how to make oil, gummies and salve infused with cannabis from some wonderful witchy friends. I became an advocate for the use of cannabis, which didn't always sit right with everyone.

People unfriended me and blocked me, talked negatively about me behind my back, But I continued to speak my truth. Eventually, the truth always comes out, and now the research is proving what I knew all along. That cannabis is a medicinal herb that has been given to us by the creator so that we can have optimal health. We all have a cannabinoid system that only cannabis attaches to. We were meant to consume cannabis, and 100 years ago, we did. Queen Victoria used it for her menstrual cramps. Hemp was a common product found in rope, clothing, etc. and yet today, you would be hard pressed to find a hemp farmer. Hemp grows at a faster rate than trees and is much stronger and more sustainable than wood, yet we aren't growing it. Why is that? It usually boils down to money and greed.

I am glad that I had the courage to colour outside the lines and give Chloe cannabis oil to ease her symptoms and prolong her life, and it truly did. She lived twice as long as the vet said she would, and she stopped peeing so much and had a trusty companion in Simon. She too was euthanized when she became too ill and is buried with Babe, Shamus, Kodi and Simon in the Forget Me Not Garden. A stray cat, a family member's cat, a homeless lady's dog and a rabbit are also buried in this sacred place I call home.

Don't be afraid to go against the grain of society. Doctors don't know anything about natural remedies and aren't even taught about cannabis. Psychiatrists are still saying that it causes schizophrenia when it does not. Many people with that disorder use cannabis because it helps them, and the truth is, we don't even know what the cause of schizophrenia is. Childhood trauma is most likely the culprit as is environmental health (heavy metals) and genetics. Cannabis has been blamed for causing addictions it doesn't cause and thousands of people have been incarcerated unfairly just because they used it. Some people are allergic to it and having too much oil can cause paranoia and panic attacks. The dose and strain for the conditions it helps vary.

Chloe showed me the way, and I am so grateful that I had the honour to care for her in her final years on this earth. Dote on the people in your life, the way that I doted on Chloe. Show love to those who love you and even to those who don't. Remember that there will always be people who hate you. It's not you that they hate. It is your light that they hate. Keep shining anyway. They aren't ready to come out of the darkness yet, and you don't have to convince them. Just move on.

Key Takeaway - The Lesson

Speak your truth even if those around you are critical of it. Eventually, the truth always comes out and you will be vindicated, but by the time that happens, you won't care anymore. Learn not to care what other people think. Learn to smile and nod. Don't get pulled into other people's drama. Remain in the now, calm, cool and collected. These are the lessons I have learned from these amazing dogs.

I have also learned to accept love in every form that it comes, even if it means a person who is 25 or 74 or 44, age truly doesn't matter when we are enlightened to our own divine power and light. Keep shining in the midst of the storm because everyone needs a lighthouse sometimes. Dogs, horses, birds and even squirrels are my lighthouse.

Chapter 6:
Simon Says, Love Is All You Need

Every single dog that I have had the honour of caring for, has been very special to me, but this little beagle took the cake. Not only did he cause intense arguments with my spouse and, subsequently, my daughter, he also ruined a wall that had to be torn down and dug holes all over the place and, he was sick.

Upon discovering that he had heartworm, my daughter paid $1000.00 over many months to make him well. My husband didn't think that dogs should ever be on our beds, but I snuck Simon on the bed every chance I got. He worked late hours helping everyone else in the world, so

I was left alone, a lot. Simon and I cuddled often and I took videos of him quietly snoring. I can't even watch them now. He brought a deep peace and an unwavering sense of loyalty and love to my life.

Beagles are known to be runners. They are primarily used for hunting, but beagles have also been used in the cosmetic industry for many years. Kept in small cages, they are experimented on so that we can have makeup. It makes no sense to me. We suspect this may have happened to him as he was branded, and he was extremely afraid of men. My husband was never able to pet him as he would scurry away from him whenever he approached. He stopped approaching because it agitated him to think that a dog didn't like him, but Simon really didn't. It wasn't until a week before he died that he submitted to my husband and laid at his feet.

I, for one, was shocked and delighted that they had made their peace with each other, but it was a little too late. A short week later, Simon was struck and killed instantly by a white truck that was speeding to get to work. At least he stopped.

It was my husband's birthday, and I was cooking him a special breakfast when I let Simon and Chloe out to pee as I always, did but this time, they were at the mailbox across the street. I went out and scolded them and brought them back in the house. I continued making the breakfast. Maybe 30 minutes later, they were asking to go out again, and I absentmindedly let them both out. Not thinking that they were grounded for going to the mailbox. Distracted because it was my husband's birthday and I was focused on making the perfect breakfast for a man for whom even perfection isn't good enough.

I was in the bedroom for a minute when he came rushing in and said Simon and been hit and it didn't look good. I ran outside, and the guy said he was gone. He placed him at the side of the road. I thanked him and apologized for my dog being in the way of his truck and causing him his own trauma. All of a sudden, an immense feeling of peace rushed over me and I turned and went back into the house to get a blanket for my beloved dog. As I was searching, I remember thinking "Why am I so calm right now? I should be hysterically crying, but I am not." The neurofeedback I had been doing for C-PTSD was working. It trains your brain to remain calm.

I found a blanket and went to the road. Blood was smeared at the end of our driveway and there he lay, lifeless. I picked him up and could feel the warmth of his body as I carried him to the Forget Me Not Garden to be buried alongside his dearest friends. My husband dug the grave as I called my daughter who was away visiting a friend to tell her the awful news. She blamed me of course. She had a premonition that Simon was going to be killed by a vehicle, and she blamed me for not taking better care of him. She wasn't wrong. I blamed myself too. If only.....

Simon was only six years old and had survived abuse and heartworm, and on this day, he ran straight into heaven. Chloe had been chasing him, and he looked back at her as he ran right out of the ditch into the path of a speeding white truck. Chloe almost got hit as well and would return to that same spot day after day after day. Perhaps she was wondering where Simon went.

Every single day as I go to the mailbox, I say his name out loud as I pass over the spot where he lost his life. His blood stained the road for months on end until they repaved it, and now it is gone. Chloe was the only dog left, and three months later, she too went home, and they are all buried facing the west, as the sun set upon their lives.

Simon showed me what true love is. He showed me how to play and keep that youthful spirit. He showed me that he loved and appreciated me as I did him, and there is no better feeling in the world than to know that you are loved, especially when most of your life, you didn't.

Simon was always darting in front of me at the speed of light, scaring me in the process. I think it was his way of playing with me. He had so much energy and was such a bright light in my life. I was thankful to have Chloe, but she too left me only a few short months later, and I remained without a dog for three years until the pandemic hit and I bought myself the dog I have always dreamed of owning: a bernese mountain dog I named Lola.

Key Takeaway - The Lesson

If you have lost your childlike spirit, now is the time to find it, and having a dog will help you tremendously. Dogs love to play and help us to get in touch with the innocence that was perhaps taken away far too young. A dog is trustworthy, beyond what humans are capable of. Find a friend that will defend you when you aren't there, who will love you through every experience in your life and who will always be there, ready, willing and panting to go on an adventure with you. There is no greater love than the love dogs give to us. Isn't that what they say about Jesus?

Dogs and horses help to show us how to remain in the now where there are no problems or worries. They live in the present but are always aware of the potential harm that could befall them. They are aware, but not bothered. They are peaceful, and just being with them lowers your heart rate. Take the time to find the peace that you didn't have as a child. Learn to truly love your inner child by taking care of you first. So many of us who have lived with childhood trauma (Chronic Post Traumatic Stress Disorder or CPTSD) give so much to others because we know what it feels like not to receive the love that we all need resulting in feeling chronically alone and hurting. We forget about ourselves and eventually become burnt out because we are not taking care of ourselves first and foremost. This is one of the greatest lessons I am learning now. To put myself first, for a change, then everything good follows.

Chapter 7:
And Then There Was Lola

I knew that Bernese mountain dogs were $2500.00 – $3000.00, and I didn't have that kind of money to spend on a dog, and they rarely came into animal shelters. I found Bernese mountain dog puppies mixed with Pyrenees and thought what a perfect blend. They were both herding dogs that are great on a farm. They were $1100.00 and located not too far from Oakville where I would pick up my grandchildren. I made arrangements to pick her up on the same day I dropped them off to their parents after one of our summer visits. It was September 6, 2021, which I remember because it was also my mother's birthday, and I thought, what a fitting gift, to celebrate my mom.

I had actually picked out Lola's sister, but when I got there, she ran away from me, and Lola came up to me and started licking my feet. She chose me, and so I brought her home. She was shaking with fear but soon settled in and, as a puppy always does, she chewed a bunch of things.

Lola is the most adorable and loving dog I have ever had. She was born on June 30, 2021 and will be three years old this year. This dog is so smart. I have been training her off leash, and even though sometimes she takes off on me, she always returns when I call her. Lola knows when I am sad and will come over and start licking me and nuzzling me. She is so attuned to me that she leaps into action at the slightest hint of noise. Many are terrified of her as her bark and growling are ferocious. I know that female dogs are much more loyal than male dogs, so I made sure to get a female.

She is a natural defender. Lying in front of my three miniature horses, Lola is their guardian and she knows it. She met them through the fence for the first few years, but I can tell that they are friends now. She helps to get them back into the corral after I let them out for a bit of grass. I was a bit worried about having another dog since I took in an American bulldog in 2020, and he got loose and chased and bit the horses. It was an awful day, and I had to surrender him to the humane society. He ended up with a family through Bullies In Need, a dog rescue that specializes in bulldogs. He couldn't be with any other animals but was incredible with children. I suspect that he was used in dog fights. He had my horse Ruby by the neck and would not let go. I punched him in the nose, and he released her and instantly came back to himself and sat down.

Everyone who meets and gets to know Lola falls madly in love with her. She is the kind of dog who will come up to you and lay her head on your lap and look up at you with her dark brown eyes. She provides comfort to anyone who is sad, as she is a highly sensitive dog. I have never had a dog who is so connected with the people around her. Lola teaches me to remain in the NOW.

When I am walking her on the trail, she will stop and look and listen. I stop too and take in whatever it is she is sensing. It is in these moments, when we are connected in nature where the divine lives where there is no stress, no problems, no hang ups, no worries. The trick is to remain in that moment and not fall back into the past where we will find depression or worry about the future, where there is anxiety.

Lola also loves car rides! Sometimes she will sit by my vehicle, waiting for me to open the door. She loves to stick her head out the window and take in all of the scents. For the first two-and-a-half years of her life, she spent at least two days a week with other dogs at various doggie daycare centers. She loves playing with other dogs; it is people she is not overly fond of, simply because she hasn't been exposed to many. Whenever someone comes to visit, they have to first get through the Lola test. If she doesn't like you, she will bark and growl no matter how much I tell her no. She knows the energy of a person far better than I do. The horses are the same way. They feel us and then start acting like we do, but that is another book.

Lola, like all dogs, has taught me what true love looks like. She is always so happy when I come home and follows me everywhere I go. She will lick me to show me how much she adores me and cuddle with me in my bed. Some people think it's weird to allow a dog in the bed because they think they are dirty. A little dirt never hurt, and Lola always lies on top of the covers. I can always wash the blanket that she lies on, but having a sweet, furry, dog cuddle up to you is one of the most blissful feelings in the world.

Don't be pulled into the opinions of others. Get yourself a dog that you can cuddle with. Over the many years that I saw people in my private practice as a psychotherapist, my dogs have been the ones who have provided comfort to those who are hurting. Both Babe and Chloe would sit on the feet of the person who was the most troubled, and it was always a touching moment for them.

I left the field of psychotherapy and social work a few years ago after realizing that talking about your problems is not the way to heal. Talking helps us to understand why we do the things that we do, but, after a lifetime of being both a patient and a practitioner, I know that it doesn't bring true healing. Not only that, it is expensive, and many people don't have the resources to pay to see a therapist every week. Even if they do have the resources, like through extended health benefits, they are always limited.

Spending time alone, in nature, with animals does bring healing, and I am a prime example. I recently had some reiki done and the woman told me that all of my chakras were balanced. I couldn't believe it. Finally, I am balanced. I worked very hard to get to this place, and even my doctor says that my onion is almost finished peeling. We are like onions when we are working on our trauma. There are layers and layers and layers of abuse and false beliefs that we have adopted throughout our lives. Dogs help us to peel back the layers and get to the core root of our issues.

Dogs are excellent in a crisis, which is why I can't for the life of me understand why, when my mother died, they sent my dog away, at I time, when I needed her the most. After she died, we were sent to her parents' house in the USA to visit them for two weeks every summer. My grandfather was a lively man who told dirty jokes and was the life of the party. He also became my molester and I dodged that man for years. He bathed me and my sisters and would expose himself to us and touch us inappropriately. He kissed us with wet kisses that were way too long and very uncomfortable. When I started developing breasts, he grabbed at them every chance he got. I was so confused that I finally told my grandmother what was going on when I was 10 years old.

I had found his pornographic magazines under his easy chair and was shocked when I looked at them. I gave them to my grandmother and told her that he forced me to touch his penis while sitting with him in his chair. He pushed my hand down, in between his legs and exposed his penis, and then squeezed his legs together. I was in a full blown panic and froze. I didn't cry out or run away. I froze. My grandmother was sitting right there, beside us, and she didn't even notice. Upon learning about this disturbing event, she said that he was impotent. I didn't even know what that meant, but it sounded like an excuse.

I was very close with her, and sitting on a little and uncomfortable stool beside her was my safe place. My sister was always sitting with him, while my other sister always sat on the couch. She was lucky, because he couldn't touch her there. I don't know how I ended up in his chair that day because I always tried to stay far away from him, but I did. When I asked my sister if he had done the same to her, she said that he had. Upon sharing with my older cousin, my Auntie Em overheard me and confronted me. My sister got really upset and said that I was lying. When my dad asked me about it, I naturally protected my sister by saying that I was lying, but I wasn't. I never understood why she would defend a perpetrator. She even had him walk her down the aisle at her first marriage to the abusive man who fathered her three children.

Childhood trauma follows you all the days of your life. Sometimes a smell or a song will trigger you back to the moment when you were being abused, and there is nothing that you can do about it. I have learned to ride the waves of these disturbing memories and cling to my dog who truly makes me feel safe and loved. I can honestly say that Lola is my very best friend who is always there for me whenever I need her. I can't say that about any person in my life.

Key Takeaway - The Lesson

You can always trust your dog, or your horse for that matter. They will never lead you astray. Learning to trust after a lifetime of betrayal is easy with an animal because they are inherently good. They won't hurt you. You will get in their way perhaps and get hurt, but they won't try to hurt you. Everyone else in life will. Learn to depend on and love yourself first. I can't stress that enough. It took me 50 years to start loving myself, and it has taken me to great heights, ones I would have missed had I not.

Give extravagantly to yourself, to your pets, to others. Be a giver, not a taker. Dogs give and give and give and are ready to give some more. Open your heart and know that as you give, you will also receive.

Chapter 8:
Dogs Show Us How to Love

Is there anything better in this world than a dog showing you so much excitement when you arrive at home? Do your family or loved ones get as excited when you return home as your dog does? Highly unlikely.

Does anyone lick your face or your feet because they are so ecstatic to see you? Does anyone come and lay their head on your lap and stare at you with the most mesmerizing eyes? Does anyone come to your defense, even if they have no idea what the situation is? Humans will always let us down with dogs, on the other hand, never do. They are ready, willing and able to go on an adventure, sit with us as we mourn, defend us to the death and love us into eternity. They are so very loyal. Dogs will never be disloyal to us like people are. They are just the most perfect companions, and we can learn a lot from them.

Dogs are like God on earth. I truly believe that dogs were created not for us to use like in racing, dog fights or dog shows, but to teach us about love. How pure and unadulterated they are. Dogs are a best friend that always has your back. Research has shown that men are more successful at getting a girl's phone number if they have a dog with them. Studies have also shown that dog owners have less of a chance of having heart, cholesterol and high blood pressure issues. Dogs provide us with emotional support and help us to feel less lonely.

Most dog owners view their dog as part of the family, and many love them more than their spouse. I can understand that. Lola would growl at my husband when she knew he was in a bad mood. She would run ahead of him and get in front of me so that he couldn't come near me. She knew instinctively that he had negative energy, and even though he pretended to like her, she knew the truth.

Gazing into the eyes of your dog triggers the release of oxytocin, the love hormone, and when we spend quality time with a dog, this boosts levels of dopamine, the mood hormone. They reduce our stress and anxiety and can even sniff out diseases like cancer. Pet owners are more likely to interact with other people too. They actually make us more attractive to prospective partners. They also force us to get out of bed and take a walk with them several times a day. They are the perfect anti-depressant and anti-anxiety medication.

Dogs have a lot to teach us if we would only pay attention. They provide us with unconditional love. Dogs spend their lives trying to show us what love is. They become our family and our most trusted friends. When we can't find it among humans, we will find it with our dogs. They sense what we are going through and they are very patient with us. There is a connection that is incredible. The way we speak to our dogs is the same way, we need to speak to ourselves. Words like "good girl, I love you so much, you are the best." They are angels that are sent to us at just the right time. They show us how to be compassionate, to ourselves and others. Forgiveness, acceptance and love are just some of the positive aspects that dogs bring to us.

I believe that when you go through childhood trauma, oftentimes it creates in us a great level of empathy and compassion. We have such a keen understanding of neglect, abandonment and rejection that we live our lives thinking and feeling about other people, sometimes even more than ourselves. There is a great book called "Women Who Love Too Much" by Robin Norwood, which talks about this. We develop this need to overdo things, like loving too much, talking too much, caring, too much. Many times my husband told me that I needed to learn to care less.

That is a very difficult thing for an empath to do. Dogs never care less. Dogs always care about their owners and never change their minds. Dogs don't reject or abandon us, as we do them. The shelters are full to overflowing with unwanted dogs. I didn't want to buy my dog from a breeder but I was unable to find a Bernese mountain dog at the shelters. Probably because they are such an amazing breed, fewer people get rid of them. We dispose of dogs in such heartless ways. Dogs will never dispose of us. They will always be there for us even if we ignore them. They are always waiting for our attention and love.

A dog simply will never let you down. True love is walking into the room and, upon seeing you, your loved one says "I'm so glad that you are here," or they wag their tail. Same thing, different species. All of my dogs were, so very loyal to me. They loved me just as I am. They didn't expect much from me but food, a little belly rub now and then, and shelter from the storm.

I was honoured to be the one they chose to feel safe with. Much like my youngest daughter, who was attached to my hip from birth to age nine when we finally broke loose and found our freedom.

Free from the constant anxiety of living with someone who could blow up at any given minute. The "walking on eggshells" for years were finally over, and it must have been a great relief to her, since it was, sadly, all that she had ever known.

I was the one she knew she could turn to and depend on to keep her safe, no matter what. Isn't that what a parent is supposed to do? I was the one who she could count on.

I will always be loyal to my children and to those who are loyal to me. The rest, well, life is too short to repair relationships that only prove over and over again to be toxic. Unfortunately, family and friends will let us down, disappoint us and even stab us in the back. If anyone came near me in an aggressive manner, my dogs would attack without command; they would attack out of love and loyalty.

To be loyal is to be faithful, devoted, dependable and constant. Dogs are all of these things and so much more. It would truly be a gift to find one person who would be as loyal to me as my dogs have been. I am protective and watchful over those whomI love and suspicious of those who want to hurt me or my loved ones. I believe that this is wisdom, and I learned it from these incredible creatures.

Dogs instinctively know when we are sad and try to comfort us. When someone is sad, sit close to them and be there when they are ready to receive your love. No words need to be spoken; nuzzle close and just be with the person, walking in their shoes and feeling the pain they are experiencing. That is what every one of my dogs would do whenever I was sad. They just knew. When a man can't figure a woman out, it takes a dog to show them the way.

My four grandchildren live a seven hour drive away from me, but we see each other on the computer, and I drive down every few months to pick them up and bring them back to Computer Grandma's house in the country. That's what they used to call me, and when they were small, they would try to hug and kiss me through the computer. When I haven't seen them for a few months, they run toward me, arms spread out wide, huge smiles on their faces, and I do the same. Then I scoop them up into my arms, and their arms find their way around my neck and there is no better feeling in the world! That's the kind of welcome our dogs give us every time we walk in the door.

That is the same way I felt every time I saw Kodi getting up and moving as quickly as she could toward me, to say hello and that she is happy that I am home. It is a feeling of love and happiness and of complete and pure joy!

My mother's tombstone reads: ***Weeping May Endure For The Night But Joy Cometh In The Morning, Psalm 30:5***. I was puzzled as to why my father would choose that scripture. Did he really think that we could ever experience joy again after such a tragedy? Well the scripture is right, joy does come in the morning. Things always look darkest before the dawn. The night time has a way of bringing out our fears and sadness but the sun will shine again and there will be joy again. It may not be the next day; it may be weeks, months and even years before joy is felt again, but it will come.

I have sat with countless people as they faced their own immortality due to an incurable cancer, and it is sad and frustrating beyond belief because there is nothing that they can do, nothing anyone can do. After trying chemotherapy and radiation, some people just wait to die while others learn how to live. Finding joy and gratitude in everyday moments is the key to lasting happiness.

We often overlook the joy of having a family, a career, a home and close friends. Look first to bring more joy into your immediate surroundings, with the people who you are the closest to, for the day will come when you are separated. Many people volunteer countless, selfless hours helping others while neglecting the people at home. We often take out our frustration and anger on the people closest to us, namely our spouse, children and family. It is these relationships that are most important. These are the relationships that need to be nurtured.

Many people may find themselves estranged from their family for one reason or another. I know that there are times when it is indeed better to have no contact with a family member who is abusive or undermines your self-esteem and confidence. Often, friends become closer than family, and these relationships can be just as strong and fulfilling as the ones with our family.

I have also met seniors who have lost all of their friends and family and are alone. There are countless seniors living in long-term-care facilities who never get a visit from anyone, because there is no one. We can be the light in that person's life; we can bring them joy. Even though they are at the end of their life, there is still joy to be found. Find ways to show love to everyone who surrounds you. Our dogs' priority never changes; they always want to be near us.

Alzheimer's runs in my family, and I had to sit and watch helplessly as my Auntie Em slipped into its grasp. She was locked up for a year, and I'm sure it was the worst year of her life. It absolutely killed me not to be able to rescue her from her prison. So, I decided to do what I could by immersing myself in Montessori Methods for Alzheimer's and Dementia.

The number of seniors grows every year, and the number of people being diagnosed with Alzheimer's and Dementia has skyrocketed. With all of the advances in medicine, people are living longer than expected. Auntie Em lived to be 91 before she passed away. Her last year on Earth was her worst, and although I tried to rescue her, I couldn't. I wasn't the one in charge. Had I been, things certainly would have been a lot different.

First and foremost, I would have taken her back to the only city she had ever known, London, Ontario, where she was born and raised, where she lived and raised three children and three little nieces who needed her more than she ever knew. I would have spared no expense and gotten her the best treatment and care money could provide. She would have lived like a Queen, being waited upon, but there would always be room for her in the kitchen if she chose to cook. I can't imagine how many wonderful meals that dear soul made for me over the years. After every meal, she would say, "Well there's a cavity filled." She would continue to be active, but with things that she enjoyed doing, even if it was going to the Casino!

These days, there are not enough rooms in the inn for the number of seniors who require care. Many seniors are tied up in their wheelchairs so that they won't fall out and hurt themselves, a method that is easier for the caregiver but gives the client no dignity. Believe me, it doesn't matter whether you spend 10,000 dollars every month for a long-term care facility, or how fancy it may appear, it doesn't mean that your loved one is getting the best possible care. That became glaringly true when I visited Christine, a former colleague, who I had known for decades.

I was granted permission to visit her, and she was now in late stage Alzheimer's. Her sister told me that she was frail, mute and in the end stages in the summer of 2023. I brought all of my Montessori activities with me. It was a glorious two hours when she spoke and smiled and came back to life, if only for a while. I found her slumped over, tied in with a seatbelt in a wheelchair, by the window at a fancy "memory care" facility. Her husband boasted that he paid a lot for it and that he could afford it. He also told me that he visits for four hours every week. One hour a day for four days. Out of 168 hours a week, he sees his wife of decades for four of them or 6% of his time. He is an arrogant man, and meeting him made me realize that her life wasn't as perfect as she made it out to be.

Montessori seeks to encourage life rather than give up on it and to use what you do have and not what you have lost to maintain a role within your community, which gives you dignity and hope. Research has shown that this method decreases the need for anti-anxiety medication (which, by the way, is extremely addictive and has side effects such as drowsiness). Do we really want our seniors to sleep the rest of their lives away just because their brain isn't working like it used to?

I am committed to this road because of my Auntie Em, who was stuck in a long-term care facility, with nothing to do and no one to help her. Even though I wasn't able to get her out of that place and was powerless against her power of attorney, I didn't give up, not ever, just so she could live the rest of her life in dignity and in peace. Instead, she was tormented and broken in the end and left sooner than she should have, but I don't blame her. I am glad that she doesn't have to endure that anymore, but I am angry that it happened at all. It is because of her that I embrace this challenge, which is to teach everyone else how to bring dignity back to Alzheimer's and dementia patients. Who knows, one day, it could be you!

Her older brother suffered from the same thing, but it will not come after me! I am determined to do whatever I can to stay mindful and healthy in body, soul and mind. Did you know that dancing good for our brains? I have started to dance again.

I was angry that no one in my family had told me that she was near the end, because I would have hopped in my car and driven the five to six hours to see her before she slipped away. She died the day after my 47th birthday. My Dad called to tell me the news. I knew something was really wrong because he never called me - his wife always did. I dreaded those phone calls in which I would be stuck on the phone for at least an hour as she talked and talked and talked some more. I truly believe that Auntie Em waited an extra day to make sure not to die on my birthday because then every year I would be sad instead of celebrating my birth.

I was so torn up and broken inside that I cried out that day, looking out my window, asking her why she had to go and how could I go on without her? Truly one of the most miserable days of my life, so broken that I didn't get a chance to say good-bye to the only mother I had ever known and loved. Her death shook me to the core. And then I saw it, the bird, a sparrow, caught in the bird feeder outside my dining room window.

My heart leapt for this helpless bird flapping furiously trying to get out of its glass cage. I ran outside and opened the lid, and the bird flew out but it didn't fly away. It flew around me in a circle three times, then, stopped and landed on the bird feeder inches from my face and looked into my eyes, while I looked into its. "Auntie Em?', I questioned out loud. "Yes it's me, I came to say good-bye, please don't be sad because now I am free! I love this place where you live and I like your car (1963 Red Valliant parked in the driveway). I am happy that I got to see it. I'm going home now to be with your mom and we will be waiting for you! Don't be sad. There is lots more for you to do before it is your time." And off she flew.

I know what you are thinking: I must be crazy, and sometimes I wonder, but this truly happened to me, and it was the first day that I realized how much I can sense spiritual things, how much I have always been connected to heaven and how much my mother has been watching over me from beyond. I wouldn't even recognize her voice if I heard it, or would I? They call it the sixth sense, and it makes sense to me. As a creative arts therapist, I utilize all of the five senses and am learning more each day about this other spiritual connection that has been with me all along!

God, The Creator, The Universe's eye is not only on the sparrow, but it is on all of us.

Key Takeaway - The Lesson

The key to happiness in life is to operate from love. Love like a dog. Think about it. Show enthusiasm when your significant other returns home. Kiss them, hug them, tell them that you are happy to see them. It's when we allow fear to seep in that trouble comes. Fear is what stops us from creating the amazing lives we were always meant to create. So many people live in fear; they call it anxiety, they call it panic. It is all the same thing. It is operating from fear. Try transitioning to love, and start with showing love to yourself. Only you know what true love feels like for you. The Five Love Languages are a great place to start.

Affirmations, Acts of Service, Quality Time and Touch and Gifts are the five ways that we send and receive love, and one often speaks louder than others. Give love to yourself, and then you will be full enough to be able to share with others

_____

Chapter 9:
Dogs Know How to Wait and When to Take Action

I do feel like I have been spending my entire life Waiting for a better job, or a better partner, waiting in line to get food, waiting to be served, waiting on others to catch up, waiting for the bus, waiting for love...to arrive. When you come from childhood trauma, love is foreign to you. What you know is neglect and abuse, but you mistake them for love. You even mistake sex for love. It's challenging to grow up believing these crazy things like that we aren't loveable because we are, or that there is something wrong with us, because there isn't. We love to label everything from mental health problems to genres of movies and music. Heck we even label children and animals spoiled, lazy or special needs. Everyone has a box. Me, I live in the white female of Irish and Scottish decent survivor of childhood trauma, advocate of nature and animals to heal, cannabis advocate and patient box (that one always gets me in trouble but at this age, I welcome the trouble.) I welcome it because it always comes, so instead of fighting it, I welcome it, knowing that whoever said "this too shall pass" was right because it always does. Change is happening every moment of our life. Those who resist it are those who suffer the most.

I finally decided that I am going to stop waiting for the bus that never arrives. You know the old saying, that if you keep trying to do things the same way you have always done them and expect different outcomes, that is a sure sign of insanity? Well, I finally got it, and I am not waiting for anyone anymore. But for my dog, I will wait. Because our dogs wait for us all day long to come home from the rat race, we call work.

Dogs know how to wait. They curl up and have a nap in the sun, or under a tree, heck, some will even dig a hole and lay down in it to keep cool. Dogs know how to wait. People, not so much. People rush around all day "working," rush to get there and rush to get home, rush to get the children and partner fed not to mention themselves, rush to an activity, rush home, rush to bed and get up and do it all again. Very few people take the time to sit down and wait.

Wait, really wait. Be quiet. For five minutes. Try it. Right now.

I'll wait.

Prayer is talking to God, the Creator, Allah, Jesus, Mary, Hari Krishna, Bob, John, but meditation, meditation is listening to the divine. The problem is, so many people aren't listening at all. Many healers spend hours in meditation and in nature with animals in order to help others to heal from similar tragedies.

Learning to wait is what life is all about, but there does come a time, like years of waiting for someone to ask you to marry them, when the waiting is done. Many have left after waiting more than a decade. Waiting for a child to be born that never comes and then waiting to find a way to become a parent. Waiting for immigration to say that you can stay or for the doctor to tell you it's not cancerous and thank goodness you had the test. It saved your life. Prevention is everything.

Lola will wait for hours; she will lie by the door, and sometimes on the bed. Often she is found right beside me, at my feet. Which reminds me of a story I must share here. A story of a man who is telling other men to wash their women's feet. I was researching him for an interview I was doing for the Ottawa Grassroots Festival and I read his blog and the fact that a man would encourage other men to show such a beautiful sentiment of love, moved me.Most men I know would say, "She can do it first." This man was onto something I have been waiting for. There I go, waiting some more. You can find his blog at www.albertdumont.com

There does come a time when the dog is finished with waiting and they must move into action, but learning to wait, to be still, to appreciate the present moment, is a skill that needs to be taught and practiced by all of us. Lola won't stop pestering me when it's time to go outside. There does come a time when waiting is no longer an option and we must act.

This is a season of acting for me. I have waited long enough. None of us knows how long we have on this earth, so it's time to rise up and take action. We can't wait for the government to care about the homeless; we have to take care of them ourselves. We can't wait for immigration to accept people who are coming from war; they need our help now. We can't wait for him to come and pick up his things because he isn't coming. He is only playing with you, again. So, keep moving.

As I look out my window, I see my three miniature horses, and they are all lying down in a circle. It's only 9:30 a.m. and this is a rare occurrence to see. Oppie got up and is standing watch over the other two, basking in the sun. Emmie has her head lowered on the ground. These majestic animals brought me true healing, much like the dogs, but in a completely different way. These three showed me myself. They bring out the dark and the light in us because they are highly intuitive and feel what we are feeling, even if we don't know what we are feeling.

Addiction occurs because the person is trying not to feel unloved, unworthy or like a failure. A person becomes addicted to something because they don't want to feel the negative emotions from their traumatic childhoods. Addiction is actually a survival instinct. Can you imagine being penniless without a home or even a pillow to rest your head? Imagine living outside, in all kinds of weather, and, at the mercy of others, for food? Do you think that would be enjoyable? Of course not, and most of us would not survive, but many, many, many, do. It's getting worse because we are all so disconnected. and the only way to heal is to reconnect with the divine that is within all of us. The divine is in plants and animals and the wind and the sun and the moon. Lola is a herding dog, as were Chloe and Babe before her, and they instinctively know that their job is to protect the horses and they do. Each one, in their own way, would lie in front of the gate where the horses live, to keep watch over them. The horses do the same for each other. They are sisters, and although they can be seen fighting especially at breakfast and dinner over the hay, there is always one standing when the other two are laying down. They have each other's backs, and that is the most beautiful act of love there is.

Key Takeaway - The Lesson

There is a time to wait and a time to act, but love, love is always an action. Love isn't just words, love is doing, it is pleasing, it is kind and nourishing. It is sometimes doing something that we don't really want to, but we do to make someone else happy. Just make sure you do the same for yourself. Learn to love the waiting because that is when there is the most peace. Embrace the times when life is slower, and don't try to rush anything because timing is, indeed, everything.

Take time to nourish the relationships that are the most dear to you. Those relationships that pour into your life and leave you wanting more. Make your dog a priority in your life - you won't be sorry. Your relationship with your dog is one of the most sacred.

Love fearlessly; love like your dog.

Chapter 10:
Sit With Me

Sometimes, all that we really need is someone to hold space for us. Someone who is trustworthy and nonjudgmental, who will simply sit and be with us, as we go through the negative emotions of life. Many people want to fix us and will make suggestions for things that we can do to improve our circumstances, but oftentimes that isn't what we need.

Dogs know instinctively what we need, and they are happy to give it to us. Holding space for someone is very sacred, and it is at the heart of all therapy sessions. When someone is able to simply listen and provide their support, that is such a blessing, but humans always have their own idea of what that looks like. Dogs simply sit with us. They don't judge us. They show us love in the darkest of times.

In order to hold space for someone, you must be comfortable with silence. So many people rush through their day, never taking the opportunity to sit in silence and listen to the voice within. This is the main problem with our modern society. Everyone thinks that we must be working every second of every day in order to be successful but, learning to rest is just as important, if not more so.

Dogs know how to rest. They are not running around all day long. Dogs know how to sit with us and just be. They are comfortable with silence. They are always in the NOW. Next time you take your dog on a walk and they stop and stare in silence, just be with them and take it all in. You will feel the amazing sense of peace that they always bring to us.

When I worked as a social worker, I held space for people all the time. It is a skill that you can learn. Not offering advice, but simply actively listening, paying attention to every word, without judgment or offering your opinion. Allowing a person to share their story with kindness and respect is one of the most loving things that we can do. Dogs do this all the time and yet so many people can't spend one quiet moment reflecting on their life.

I teach Stress Management at Healing Minis Farm School and always teach about meditation. So many students believe that they can't meditate because they are unable to quiet their mind. If you struggle with the inability to quiet your mind, then that is a sign that you need to learn how to mediate. Getting rid of all of the thoughts isn't the goal. Sitting in silence and listening to the voice that is within each of us is. Prayer is talking to the creator, and meditation is listening.

It reminds me of a beautiful song that my friend Angel Forrest wrote for her husband, Denis, called, Listen. The lyrics are:

"Listen, I want you to listen. I want to tell you who and all you are to me my friend. You pick me up and you dust me off. You hold me close till I shake it off. All you say and all you do,

how can I repay my soul to you? Listen, I need you to listen. I need to tell you what and all you mean, to me my love. Touch me, oh when you hold me. You silence all the screams that lie deep within, you're healing me. You pick up and you dust me off. You hold me close till I shake it off. All you say and all you do, how can I repay my soul to you? I want to know why you love me so. Do you realize that you're saving me, you're saving my dying soul? I must have done something right somewhere, somewhere along the road. With all your saying, all you're doing, how can I repay my soul to you?"

Listen, By Angel Forrest from Mother Tongue Blues.

She wrote it for her beloved husband, Denis, but it could easily be about a dog. My dog saved me. My dog picks me up. My dog loves me like no other. My dog comforts me. My dog will never leave me. The only time that my dog hurts me is when they die.

My dogs have always been there for me, unlike humans. Just the other day, I was talking with someone, and as I shared the horrors of what my husband recently did (threatened to shoot me), she replied, "Laurie, you are really bringing me down right now. I just want to focus on my music and positivity, we can catch up later." I was dumbfounded. "Ok sure yes, talk to you later then, bye," and hung up. Wow. Don't be like that.

Learn from dogs how to sit. Sit with people and just listen. I understand about being drained from other people's negative energy all too well. This person has called me numerous times in the past, drunk out of her mind, (and probably doesn't even remember it), bawling about some relationship they had managed to destroy. Alcoholism is an awful thing to live with, and I truly hope that she finds her way out of her self-centered life, but she will no longer be in mine.

I no longer have the patience for people who have no patience or care for me. I have always lived my life giving to others and very rarely has it been reciprocal. I never cared. But, I have discovered that I should care if I am constantly giving and giving and giving and never receiving anything in return. It is in my nature to give, or perhaps it comes from childhood trauma as so many things do. Dogs are givers. They give and they give and they give some more. They don't walk away from you when you are hurting. Dogs are friends on whom you can depend. And there is no truer friend than that.

Key Takeaway - The Lesson

Learn to sit, just like your dog does. Learn to sit in stillness, be quiet and just take everything in. Sit by the water and engage all of your senses. Learn how to live in the moment. Take a few minutes each day to meditate. Just sit down, close your eyes and take a few big breaths. Feel yourself relaxing a little bit more with every exhale. Do this for five minutes and then ask the questions that you have. The answers will rise up from deep within you. Dogs already know this and show us how to meditate all the time but we just don't see it because we are too busy chasing something else.

Chapter 11:
Never Give Up

In the last several years, suicide rates have skyrocketed, especially in the Northern Communities where they are cut off from the rest of the world. Suicide is never the answer. Dogs, when they know that their time is near, go off to die alone, not wanting to burden their loved ones. Dogs don't get depressed and kill themselves. Dogs do get depressed and anxious, but it is always in response to humans and how we treat them.

I lost many clients over the years to this dreadful disease, but none affected me as much as the suicide of Keith.

We met playing guitar at the local Mental Health Drop in Centre/Restaurant where "survivors" of the mental health system could hang out, play some music, write poetry, paint, participate in improvisation and other drama games, dance, colour or just sit there, soaking it all in. Utilizing the creative arts in education, in therapy and in health care settings, would become my mission statement more than 20 years later in my private practice. This is where it all began, back in 1993.

I had recently graduated with a Bachelor of Arts Honours Degree in Drama In Education from the School of Dramatic Arts at the University of Windsor in the early 1990s. In a nutshell, it was utilizing the creative arts (music, drama, literature, movement/dance and art) in education and in therapy. We devised lesson plans that included the creative arts and tested them in our local Schools and Children's Treatment Centres. It was a match made in heaven for me.

Keith larger than life, standing well over six feet tall, sandy hair, deep blue eyes and a smile that just made you feel at home. Keith was very welcoming to anyone who wanted to try to make music (even the girl who thought she could sing but sounded horrid to the rest of us because what she really did was scream). Keith, would make the time so that everyone had their chance to shine. We immediately started working together, writing lyrics and music, creating skits and scenes, listening to people's stories of being forced into psychiatric hospitals against their will, about the suicide attempts, the loneliness, the poverty, the homelessness that many lost souls in that place had experienced. Out of these collaborations grew a beautiful thing, a musical, called, "Send Me An Angel The Musical". It was born by the people who lived it every day on the street. Most, if not all, are deceased.

We were driven and worked hard rehearsing the songs, writing the story line, applying for funding, doing promo spots on the radio and visiting the psychiatric hospitals, encouraging others to join us. You didn't have to have any particular skill or ability, just a willingness to try something new, something creative. Since most of the people involved were on Ontario Disability Support Program Income Benefits due to mental health issues, we had all day every day to work on it and we did.

Like in most things, there was opposition, in a sole voice, but one that would not be silenced, another colleague who was blind with jealousy because we were doing the very thing he wanted to be doing and he hated us for it. It took away from his spotlight just as he accused me of wanting the spotlight for myself and using clients to get it. Nothing could be further from the truth.

He graduated from the same program I graduated from and even dated the Dean's daughter and was engaged to be married, until something happened that broke them up. The only male in my graduating class went on to get his Master's Degree in Drama Therapy, but he never used it in practice. He said that he didn't get paid enough to do that. I thought, "What a waste". He was wrong, but he didn't stop. He began to verbally attack and criticize everything we did, scrutinizing our every move and questioning every decision. We tried to ignore him, but when he solicited other staff to help him, we knew it wasn't going to be easy. He never did stop trying to discredit us, and in the end, he was fired. It seems what I suspected about him from the beginning was right. He was stealing from the very vulnerable clients and from the program.

Years later, shortly after I moved to the other side of the province, I received a call from this guy, apologizing for all of the crap he had pulled. Years later, after he had been fired from two jobs, he went to a 12-step program and started working the steps. When he got to number nine "make amends where you are able"my name kept popping into his head, go figure. Although I was gracious in forgiving him, it stunned me that after all these years, he finally realized all of the destruction he had caused.

He contributed to Keith's mental health in a negative way, mine as well, for many years. The apology was nice, but it came much too late to save the musical and most importantly, to save Keith. After he was fired, the whole program collapsed, the agency was no longer having "recreational therapy programs, they were divesting to the local YMCA for true integration to take place. That was that, after our bass player died from a drug overdose, fighting with a toxic colleague left, right and centre, the whole venture was over. I had recently married and gotten pregnant with my second daughter on my honeymoon, so I was pregnant and then took a year off of work. When I came back, I rarely saw Keith anymore. He had moved on to working for the Consumer Survivor Alliance and advocating for mental health rights. He became the president of the Consumer Survivor Alliance and hired homeless people to clean the office.

Keith was such a huge hearted person. He was like a big teddy bear, ready to give anyone a hug if they needed it. He would be there as a listening ear, offering a homeless person a place to stay, or a job cleaning his office. Whatever he could do to help people, he would do it. All the while, he was living as a single dad, caring for his young son who he carted around with him everywhere!

The mother of his son had her own mental health issues and together they tried to raise their son as best as they could. Keith and his boy were often together and he became a cabbie so that he had transportation, but it wore him out. He never really talked about it; he was focused on his music and the musical which has yet to be performed. He played bass on the weekends, and his son would be with his mom so Keith could work. They had their own apartments and co-parented better than most parents I have ever seen, for the sake of their adorable son.

On July 6 in 1998, while I was vacationing with my family in the Muskokas, I received a call from a colleague (and a former boyfriend, another mistake!) from work. He called to tell me, quite frankly, that Keith was dead. His roommate had found him hanging in the closet underneath the staircase. He had hung himself and taken his own life.

I was stunned, shocked, horrified and grief stricken all at the same time. Twenty-six years later, I still have not recovered from the massive sadness I feel about his passing. I wanted to run home and attend the funeral, but my then husband wouldn't think of it. Keith was a "former client" nobody worth rushing home for. I buried my grief and moved on as best as I could.

A few weeks later, I received a call from his ex-wife, the mother of his only son. She had found

Keith's journals and she wanted me to know how much he loved me and wrote about me. She wanted me to know how much I had helped him. She also told me that he took his own life because he was convinced that he had HIV and the thought that he may have (although we will never know) given it to someone else consumed him with so much grief that he killed himself. Instead of reaching out for help, he suffered alone and planned to take his own life. I should have known when he told me in the park that day.

He had sold his guitar and was giving up on music, one of the tell-tale signs that he was planning on taking his own life. I had been through so much with him that I was afraid to be even seen speaking to him in public. Keith had a case worker at the agency where I also worked and he had confided in her his feelings for me. They were unbeknownst to me, but she went behind my back and talked to my manager, who in turn, put an end to "Send Me An Angel The Musical," and after Keith's death, I couldn't even bring myself to listen to the old tapes we had made much less put on a production without him.

In a very weird twist of events, this same case worker eloped with the fellow who broke the news of Keith's death to me while I was on vacation, my former boyfriend.

I moved in with this guy, at his insistence, so that I could take a leave of absence from work and attend Teacher's College. This is the same woman who my friends from work would tell me was hitting on my live-in boyfriend every chance she could get. She can have him because he was just another alcoholic abuser. I hear that they are still happily married, and while I doubt it, I do hope so, because they deserve each other. More people I have long forgiven. At least they never had children, which I think is a good thing! Karma is real and you will reap what you sow!

It has only been in the last few years, at the urging of Keith (yes he talks to me, not every day, but he is with me, helps me, encourages me and tries to motivate me) that I have finished the script and practiced the songs we wrote together again. I am releasing the music from "Send Me An Angel The Musical" as a tribute to Keith next year as a soundtrack, and I hope to direct and produce the musical that was written so many years ago.

Despite the tragic loss of a friend and colleague so dear to me, I continue to believe in the message of the music. To never give up, to ask for help in order to keep going, to learn to have faith in yourself and trust that your life is meaningful and important. "Hold On" is one of the songs that we wrote together, and I so wish that Keith had held on, for a brighter day, but he didn't, and I shall never be the same.

Keith and I wrote eight songs together over the course of a year and a half. Even though the time we actually spent together was but a blink of the eye, he touched me in a way no one else ever has. He knows how much it broke my heart when I heard the awful news. He also knew that I believed the same way he did, that I had a heart for the homeless, just like the song we wrote, "This is For The Homeless".

He wanted to get this music out into the community so that he could get off the Ontario Disability Pension he was on due to an acquired brain injury from a motorcycle accident and support his son and send him to college. He also wanted to make sure there were programs in place like the ones I had created, for people suffering with serious mental health and addiction problems. Opportunities to write music, a book or a script, paint a picture or build a birdhouse, dance and sing, experiment with makeup and design, or quietly sell tickets for the next performance. There is a job for everyone when it comes to producing a film.

It is my greatest goal in life to see "Send Me An Angel The Musical" come to fruition. It is something that won't let go of me. It haunts me and calls me to finish it and to re-birth it into existence so that the world will know that he was here, and that he left an impressionable mark on not just my life, but on the thousands upon thousands who have yet to hear and see his talent and experience his heart. I have never met another Keith, and I don't think I ever will. He was one of a kind, and now he is the Angel who watches over me!

I have thought about taking my own life when I was in the darkest of depressions. My step-daughter, her boyfriend, his mother and his father all put formal complaints against me into the College of Social Workers and Social Service Workers for being a cannabis patient. My step-daughter took it a step further by accusing me of abuse and bullying. None of which was true. She blamed me for the fact that her inheritance from her grandfather, which my husband was the trustee of, was in an education fund that she could only access if she went to school, which she didn't.

I had to hire a lawyer and for seven years we fought the college. My lawyer was a woman who I had met from the Ladies Who Lunch Ottawa group that I was a part of at the time, and she gave me very bad advice that I followed. In retrospect, I should have listened to my own intuition because the advice backfired in a huge way and then she too abandoned me. I wanted to give up. But instead, I quit being a social worker. I just quit the college. I wonder what job she would do if she could no longer be a lawyer? She is wealthy charging $300.00 per hour, while I lost my career. Thank goodness I have a teaching degree to fall back on. I went back to school and took scriptwriting, and I am working toward producing "Send Me An Angel the Musical"as a film.

My daughter and her husband wouldn't let me see my grandchildren for nine long months after an argument surrounding the cult-like church that they attended. I wanted to die, but instead I started volunteering with babies and children. When the pandemic hit in 2020, they stopped going and have since discovered the abusive nature of this s0-called church run by my daughter's father's brother and his wife. They shunned me when I left my abusive husband and then lied to the congregation about me so that everyone else would shun me too, and they did. Every one of them, except the children, refused to speak to me.

My estranged husband threatened to shoot me in the head, and then I found the gun and reported him to the police. Just yesterday, I found the magazine and the bullets hidden in a box in the garage. He has since been arrested and is under a restraining order. For five years he fought with me over my house. The house I bought on my own when I fled my abusive first husband.

He is a hoarder, and I have been cleaning up his mess in the last nine months that he has been gone. He continues to try and steal my home from me. He has a great job making over 100 grand a year. He can afford to buy his own house but he wants mine. He isn't going to get it because if life has taught me anything, it has taught me that giving up is not an option.

Dogs will never give up on you, like people do.

Key Takeaway - The Lesson

Even if there appears to be no hope, don't ever give up. My lawyer told me that my ex-husband already paid me for my house and he has the legal right to order it sold despite the fact that he has some kind of dementia and threatened to kill me. I can't give up. I can't give in. There has to be a way to keep my house. The only way is if he agrees. He did agree but has since changed his mind. I am fighting for my home, my horses, my dog and my small business that I have worked so hard to keep. When everything around me appears to be dark and without hope, I can always rely on Lola to be there, no matter where we end up.

I was driving one day and heard "Call Sabrina." That is my sister who I haven't had any contact with in over five years. She is a legal assistant and is highly intelligent. I pushed the idea aside. The next day, I heard it again, "Call Sabrina," and so I did, and am I ever glad that I did. In one phone call, she helped me to get my confidence back. She confirmed what I knew to be true. I know exactly what to do now. He is not going to take everything from me after his family basically ruined my career, but even that is a relief. They say that the maximum time for a social worker before burnout is eight years. I had been doing it for 18 years, and it was time, because I have other things to do. I know that I am going to slay this dragon because I have my sister with me. I know our parents in heaven are rejoicing.

Chapter 12:
Love Without Conditions

We all know that dogs never put conditions on us and simply love us the way that we are. It doesn't matter to them the colour of our skin, how much money we have or don't have, who we vote for or what we believe in. Love without conditions or strings attached means that you don't expect anything in return. You just want the other person to be happy. Dogs are just like that.

In order to love unconditionally, you must be able to forgive and move past disagreements. Keeping track of the past is a sure way to distinguish any loving feelings. Not being able to admit your faults and take responsibility for your actions are signs of a narcissistic personality disorder. Unconditional love does not impose any conditions or expectations on us, and that is exactly what dogs do.

My step-mother is a perfectionist so I have been trained up in her world. It is a daunting task to overcome this disorder. Perfection doesn't exist and yet there are millions of people every single day trying to be perfect, expecting the rest of us to be as well. Quite simply, it is not only extremely unhealthy for you and the people around you, but it is abusive.

I embrace my flaws and weaknesses because without them, there wouldn't be any growth or enlightenment. I was raised in the Christian tradition that I fully adopted as my own. I taught it to my children and to many children in the form of Sunday School. Christianity has lots and lots of conditions. Love Jesus or else you are going to hell. Don't sin or else you are going to hell. Make sure you give the church all of your money or you won't be blessed. Stay with your abusive husband or else we will shun you. It is all a bunch of hogwash.

Jesus was probably the closest to perfection that there was, but even Jesus had flaws. He used a whip on a bunch of religious leaders and called them vipers. To some it meant that he was just in his anger; to others, he was abusive. Everyone comes with their own unique perspective. Accepting people just as they are is the perfection of our heart that leaders like Jesus brought to the world. Bob Marley and John Lennon said the same things that he said. Love one another, take care of your neighbour, take care of the widows and the orphans, treat your neighbour as you want to be treated. We have all heard this over and over and over again from many different prophets and yet, there is still war.

Whether we like it or not, we are social creatures and so are dogs. Dogs thrive on human interaction and will wait all day long for our return. They form strong attachments with us and just want to be in our presence. They show us love through their actions, tail wagging, licking, jumping or bringing us their favourite toy. This is the greatest lesson that dogs teach us: how to love unconditionally. They show us empathy when they sense that we are sad and attempt to comfort us in various ways.

They are loyal and forgiving, and when we interact with them, we both get a dose of the love hormone oxytocin, which is crucial in forming strong bonds, promoting social interactions and communication, and reducing stress. Clearly, dogs are excellent our mental health, so why doesn't everyone have one?

Half the world was taught that they are dirty animals that don't deserve much of our time and attention. Those are the angry people who will get sick and die early. Every living animal is a part of God, of the universe and creation. Every animal can teach us something profound. Dogs are the closest ones to us, and next are horses, who are even more intuitive than dogs are.

Every classroom, hospital room, jail cell, therapy office, would benefit tremendously from having a dog. People will come up with all kinds of excuses as to why that is a bad idea, but research has proven to us that dogs are in fact smarter than we ever will be. They lead from the heart, from the deepest part of their intuition, and they don't rely on thoughts and past behaviour to determine their present moment.

It takes practice for humans to love without conditions. It takes an enormous amount of energy to break false beliefs from our childhoods, ones like we have to be perfect or else, or we are unlovable, no one cares about us, or that we will always be lonely and sad. You know if you are a perfectionist, so please, do not pass it on to your children. Work hard to overcome it because in the end, research has shown us that perfectionism leads to disease and in particular to ALS.

Dr. Gabor Mate, in his book, "When The Body Says No," discovered that a high percentage of people who end up with this horrific disease are also perfectionists. They are high achievers who do not know how to rest and fall into the category of Type A Personality. Educate yourself and bit by bit, let things go. That's what I had to do, so I wouldn't scream at my children night and day because they made a mess. Is it ever any wonder why I ended up with three abusive men, all different types of abuse, but abusive nonetheless? And is it any wonder why I love dogs and animals so dearly because as a child, they were my only friends? The only people I knew at home were my enemies.

Leave the dishes in the sink and instead go for a walk with your dog. Let the toys stay scattered across the floor, so you can take your little one on a bike ride. Spending all of your time cleaning is only going to bring you illness. Heed my warning. Life is too short to worry so much about dirt. After you bathe your dog, they are going to go outside and roll in the dirt.

Key Takeaway - The Lesson

Learn what love is and what love isn't. This is particularly challenging if you have grown up with toxic parenting because to you, love and abuse are the same. This is the reason that so many women, like me, end up with the same abusive partner time after time after time. Some stay stuck forever. My daughter joked that I stick it out for 10 years and then I get fed up and leave. Why stay for 10 years in the first place? It always boils down to the kids.

We think that kids need two parents and that it is better than going it alone. Why are there a record number of single parents in 2024? Because marriage is a trap. Research has shown us that it is the men who benefit more from marriage than women. Any working mom can tell you how difficult it is to raise children and work by yourself, but millions are doing it and doing it quite successfully too, I might add.

You don't have to stay with an abusive partner and if you stay, because of the kids, you are bringing harm to them. If your religion tells you to stay and listen to your abusive husband, your religion has failed you. It is far better to leave so that the kids have a safe and secure home where they can heal. Staying for the children is never a good excuse to stay with an abusive partner. Find a way out because, even though it is a daunting task to do alone, there is always a way. I had to find a way out three times, and now, I am never going to have to experience that again. There are many angels along the way who will appear out of nowhere to help you. Many times it starts with you asking for help. Ask for help. Ask for help. Ask for help.

Chapter 13:
Always Be Ready For a Car Ride or an Adventure

Most dogs love to go for a car ride. You just mention those two words and their tails start to wag, their ears perk up and the excitement starts to rise within them. Enthusiasm is contagious.

Enthusiasm is all you need to get a great idea off the ground. Skill is less important because you can always find someone who has the skill that you don't have, but enthusiasm is everything and this is one of the greatest lessons from dogs. They will drop everything just to go for a ride with you.

When I was a girl, a solitary game that I played a lot was "teacher." I had a desk and a blackboard and three antique desks where my dolls and stuffed animals served as my students. I spent hours teaching them and correcting their papers. My step-mother and her sister were both teachers. I unfortunately got stuck having my step-mother as my kindergarten teacher. I was perfectly behaved of course, because if I wasn't, I would get a beating when we got home.

This led me to believe that I should be a teacher. My grandmother, who I always helped, told me that I should be a nurse, but the thought of having to work weekends and holidays let alone do the math and science required sent me in the direction of education. Education, after all, is the key to solving poverty, isn't it?

I finished my undergrad degree in Drama In Education and then majored in Dramatic Arts at Teacher's College. I graduated in 1993, when the Ontario Government was laying off teachers. I couldn't find a teaching job and I refused to look in Toronto, a big city like that never appealed to me. If I had my choice, I would have gone back to Huntsville, where I was born and where my mother is buried, but there weren't any jobs there either. I did the next best thing, which was to become a Recreational Therapist.

I worked in a program we called S.T.R.I.V.E, which stood for "Supportive Therapy and Recreation In Varied Environments". It was a fabulous program, one in which I could excel and excel I did, along with the clients I worked with. Everyone loved it. We broke boundaries and created art, music, dance and written works. We told our stories and developed the storyline when we were stopped in our tracks.

There is always a bad apple in every bunch is all I can say. A male colleague, who graduated from the same program that I did, was jealous. When you work harder than the person who works with you, well, they get pissed off because you are making them look bad. The truth of the matter is that they are making themselves look bad. I tried to lead by example, but that doesn't always work.

When the STRIVE program lost its funding after 10 years, I transitioned to becoming London's first Homeless Outreach Worker. During this time I got certified as an addiction counsellor, and in 2001 I started taking my Master of Social Work degree at Wayne State University, right across the river from Windsor in Detroit, Michigan. Many of my friends thought that I was nuts as Detroit has a high level of crime, but I fell in love with the magnificent city and loved every day that I spent there. In most of my classes, I was the only white girl.

It is extremely expensive to go to a university in a different country than your own. I applied for each year and got the Professional Graduate Scholarship, and in 2004 I graduated with honours. The girl who failed grade 9 and 10 math and barely passed in high school found her calling, or so she thought.

Fast forward 20 years and I have left the profession and am embarking on what truly brings me joy, which is music, writing and philanthropy. I am working on "Send Me An Angel the Musical"and started my own production company because quite frankly, I like being the Lady Boss. I like making my own decisions and not having to answer to other people. Arts For Life Productions will produce meaningful and educational films about various social issues, such as the housing crisis, or the dirty water on reserves, or the rising suicide rates and drug addictions plaguing our cities.

In February of 2024, I met a young man from Congo who enlightened me about the political tensions in the country and how the US are backing the rebels who are forcing the Congolese people from their homes. There are nearly 7 million people, the highest in all of Africa, who have been internally displaced by armed conflict. Wonder where they got the guns from? The great United States of America. The west has their greedy hands in the mix along with Rwanda and the Government of Congo itself. Corrupt governments abound.

I have partnered with Friends of the Congo and I will travel to Congo and meet the 800,000 mostly women and children living in the camp near the conflict. I am selling spices from a family owned Congolese company (www.fradaameck.com) who in turn donate to the camp. So far Merrickville

Food Mart is selling them. I am volunteering with Friends of Congo (www.friendsofthecongo.org) to help in the camp through counselling as many, many, many, women have been raped. Sexual assault is a weapon of war against women in Congo. Yet they are the backbone of the country.

A small group of female farmers in Lumata, DR Congo grow the Artemisisa medicinal plant that is used to fight against malaria and helps to boost the immune system. The women grow, harvest, process and package the plant into a tea that I hope to bring to Canada very soon. In return, the profits are used for prenatal care and the development and maintenance of maternity clinics near the conflict area.

I am transitioning my small business to a charity as I opened Healing Minis Farm School May 1st, 2024. I am taking everything I have learned and pouring it into Montessori-based alternative outdoor education with miniature horses. It is unique and greatly needed as our present education system is lost. Trying to control children by making them sit for hours on end, is ridiculous, and we should know better. Teachers spend most of their day telling their students to be quiet, not to run, not to climb, not to dig in the dirt.

I recently met another mentor (Peggy Taillon founder of www.heramission.org being my first). His name is Albert Dumont and he is a poet, writer, storyteller, speaker and an Algonquin Traditional Teacher. His words have taught me many things. I was asked to interview him as part of the Ottawa Grassroots Festival that I have been volunteering with for the past three years. (www.ottawagrassrootsfestival.com)

The producer is Alison Bowie, and we have become great friends and sisters from another mister. Had I not have gone out of my comfort zone and signed up for the Scriptwriting Program at Algonquin College in Ottawa, I wouldn't have had my internship at the Ottawa Grassroots Festival and I wouldn't have met Ali or Albert Dumont. My point is, always be ready to pivot, to change, to take a different road, to follow your heart.

Our dogs don't sit down and discuss whether we should go somewhere. They are up for anything and they don't complain about it. Anywhere they go with us is good for them. They love to be along for the ride. I know that the creator brought us together for such a time as this.

Key Takeaway - The Lesson

When an opportunity comes along that sparks your joy, follow it. If it brings you life, do it. If it makes you feel whole, hold onto it and go after it with everything that you have. Don't sit around and talk about it. Don't talk to everyone you know about it because you will get 10 different opinions. Get quiet and ask yourself, "What truly brings me joy, love and happiness. Find your own peace.

Dogs aren't on adventures every minute of the day. They spend most of the day sleeping and resting, but when they go, they are all in. Their enthusiasm is contagious. They don't even know where they are going or what they are going to be doing, but they trust us so implicitly that they show us they are all in. Jumping, wagging their tails, licking us are all ways that they show us their excitement. Whatever brings you that kind of excitement, do it, and do it as often as you can until it becomes your way of life.

Chapter 14:
Live in Today for Tomorrow Is Not Promised

Over the past six years, my second marriage has deteriorated to the point that it no longer even resembles a marriage. The love and commitment felt so earnestly at our wedding in Jamaica in 2008 is long gone. Mental illness has taken control of my otherwise brilliant husband. He is in another world that is full of paranoia and madness, and he believes many vile things about me. The love of my life thus far, has turned into my enemy. He uttered death threats and assaulted me and yet he pleads not guilty.

When his daughter falsely reported me to my college, out of vengeance and ignorance, we both fell into a deep depression. It was like a grenade had been thrown into our lives and we were never the same again. Although it was aimed at my head, my dear husband was injured deeply, as well as my other children, one of whom had built a wonderful relationship with her step-sister. They have not spoken since.

He dealt with his depression by working more and talking less. I cried every day for three years straight. It is very difficult to work as a Social Worker when you cannot stop crying. Our finances were affected as I was in private practice and didn't have anything to fall back on, so within a few months, I quit the job that I loved and had worked at for 10 years and applied for disability. I didn't get it. They said I was working part-time and that I had to not be working to qualify, so I stopped working for a few months and reapplied. Much to my surprise, I was accepted, but, as we all know, it is barely enough to live on.

I knew that I had to find another way to make a living, so I turned to education and to horses. I knew that animals were being used more and more in therapy, in education, in prisons and in health care settings. I was mandated to attend an appointment with a psychiatrist in Ottawa to see if I was "fit for practice." He found that I was, and even more surprisingly, he told me that whatever I was doing, I should keep on doing it because the woman he read about in this file (from a psychologist who re-diagnosed me with C-PTSD for the disability claim C standing for Complex or more than one trauma), was not the same woman who was sitting across the desk from him. I smiled and said, "I use cannabis," and left.

They put me through so much, just because I was a cannabis patient. Dogs never ever put us through anything. They are pure joy. Our families turn on us (there are some in my family who I don't even talk to anymore and I am better for it), our friends ignore our requests to get together and then post pictures on social media of their adventures with others (LWL), clients complain, students tell lies, step-children falsely report you to your employer while colleagues conspire against you. Quite frankly, the human race sucks. Thank God for dogs. I am so grateful that they remind me that even if no one else can see it, I am loved, I am divine and I am called. I am healed because of their love. I am whole because of them, not because of the thousands upon thousands of hours of psychotherapy I have gone through with countless therapists over the 40 years of my adult life. I am balanced, my chakras are aligned, my onion is peeled and I am ready to dive into the unknown.

Over the past several years I have been going to those places we are afraid to go, like to dinner, alone, or a concert, alone, or a trip to Africa, alone. We cannot wait for our perfect person to happen upon our path to do the things that bring us the greatest joy. I always believed that there was a plan and a purpose for every life, and now I realize that is not true. It doesn't matter what you do as a vocation or life choice. What matters is that you do whatever brings you the most joy and fulfillment and that you do it to the best of your ability.

Dogs always do what brings them joy. Whether it is chasing a ball or jumping in the river, dogs really know how to live. They aren't concerned about how their hair and mouths look when they stick their heads out of the window of a fast moving car. They don't dwell on yesterday or worry about tomorrow; they simply live in today. They are always present and always ready, willing and able to show us immense love. There is no one in my life who loves me like my dog.

Lola sleeps either at my feet or sometimes right beside me on my pillow, and I am so much better because of her. If a man comes along who wants to sleep in my bed with me and he opposes the dog, well, the dog will always come first. I am never going to cater to another person again. I will cater to myself and my animals and loved ones, and if you are blessed enough to be in my small circle of trusted friends, I will lavish you with my love, but I am not here to fix anyone. I am only here to remember who I am. Dogs never forget who they are. If we only learn from them, truly learn to be like them. Excitable, enthusiastic, loving and kind, they are the best example for us to follow. Dogs can show us things about ourselves that no one else can, and they always point us toward love.

Key Takeaway - The Lesson

Never stop going on adventures, having date nights or date yourself nights, like I do. Just because you don't have a partner or a friend to go with you, make sure that you show up for yourself. Tonight I am driving to Montreal to see Angel Forrest a singer-songwriter extraordinaire who I have been following for many years. I wish I wasn't going alone; sometimes it is nice to have someone else drive you, but I am blessed that I can drive and I have the means to get there. I am so happy that after many years, I get to see her and her husband, Denis, and Ricky Paquette, the amazing guitarist who works with them. I am not letting the fact that I don't have anyone in my life to go with me tonight to me, and don't you let it stop you either!

Chapter 15:
For the Love of God, Pay Attention to the Red Flags

There are always signs. Everywhere we go, there are signs. Signs from heaven showing us which way to go and signs within us that tell us when something is amiss. Our stomach starts to turn, and we feel a chill, or get really hot, our heart starts racing as we prepare to fight or flight, freeze or fawn (be overly nice). These are the body's natural built in security systems. When yours are activated too early, you spend your life ignoring them because you can't trust anyone, let alone yourself.

If you grew up being yelled at and ridiculed all the time, chances are you will end up with a partner who does the same. We gravitate toward what is familiar, even if it is abusive. Once you start to see the red flags, that is the time to move away from the person. Red flags are like a red light, and they are to make you stop in your tracks and re-evaluate this relationship. I did do that, over and over and over again, butI always made excuses for the men.

Things like, "He will get better; he just needs someone to love him. He is so funny the way he blames me for everything. I see that he was spoiled by his mother and not able to put up healthy boundaries with his ex. He only gets really mad when he drinks - that's why he doesn't drink. He found Jesus.

But now, oh now, it is completely different. I notice the red flags everywhere now and pat myself on the back when I escape another potential disaster of a relationship. Deep down inside, part of me keeps saying, "It's too late; there are no awakened and healed men in this world,and you are not going to find one." And yet I did.

The Lola test is how long she will bark at my friend before she accepts him. There have been a few who she barked at for hours, and one for whom she settled quickly and remained that way. It actually shocked me and was one of those green flags. The flags that say, this is a safe person, this is someone who you can trust, because your dog trusts him or her. This person was very calm and gentle, but lacking in other ways, like one of the most important, communication.

Lola is the security detector, she is the alarm bell ringer and she is the best friend that a woman could ever have. As I write this, she is lying on my bed, looking out the window, her head resting on my pillow. I know some of you are thinking "gross" while others are thinking "wow, so sweet". Same dog, same picture, but we all come from a different perspective. If you think it's gross, you are most likely a clean freak and a perfectionist with obsessive compulsive disorder. I know what it is like to grow up with someone with this personality disorder, and it is very damaging to those around you, let alone yourself. Remember ALS?

Dogs are even being used to detect seizures, low blood sugar levels and cancer, a lost person, drugs or a bomb. They will bark and growl at a person who they feel uneasy with or sit beside the person with the drugs. They will nudge their owner to alert them to lie down as a seizure is about to occur.

The other day, my daughter's cat, Salem, was sitting outside the door at the trailer. She is an indoor cat and strictly forbidden to go outside for obvious reasons. Lola wouldn't stop barking so I thought she needed to go out. I opened the door and there was the cat. How did she get outside? I wondered as I brought her back into the house. Lola knew she was there. Even though she couldn't see her, she sensed and smelled her.

We too can sense people who have passed on and learn to be highly intuitive. It takes practice to remember who you are. Dogs and animals never have this problem of being disconnected from themselves. Dogs and animals are always connected to the divine within. They never leave the presence of the divine. They stop, look, listen and wait. Stop, look, listen and wait are the lessons before jumping into action. That is exactly what dogs do.

Next time you walk your dog, take them to the forest and watch this occur. When they stop, you stop too and take a few deep breaths as you connect with your dog, look in the same direction, listen and wait. Wait for as long as your dog wants to wait. Your body is being flooded with natural pain killer hormones like endorphins and dopamine. In that moment, you are in the now, present with your dog. That is where God, the creator, the universe Allah, Jesus, etc. can be found.

Communication is key whether it is with your partner, children, colleagues, leaders or your dog. Granted, dogs and animals don't speak our language, but they communicate with us in many different ways. Barking, growling, lying beside us, perked ears and whimpering are just some of their communication techniques. Red flags are just that. Communication, from ourselves, that something is not right. When we grow up with red flags every single day in the form of our families, it is challenging to sort out what a red flag looks like because it is all we have ever known.

My earliest memory was when I was about three. My dad had remarried and I already was afraid of her. I was shocked that she forced us to change into our flower girl dresses for her wedding in the parking lot of the church. Yes the parking lot. Why couldn't we change in the bathroom? No, we had to change in the parking lot. At this tender age, I remember feeling mortified. In retrospect, I wonder whether the recurring dreams of being naked in public I have had most of my life are the result of this early abuse?

It was shortly after they got married and the neighbours were shooting off firecrackers. My sister and I were in bed and she was standing at the window watching the fireworks. I was wondering why we weren't outside watching them when she stormed in, grabbed my sister by her arm and started hitting her over and over and over again on her bare leg. Her long nails left a long, bloody scratch on her leg as the monster screamed, "Don't you get out of bed again", before throwing her onto the bed where she cried herself to sleep and I tried to comfort her. I hated that woman, with everything in my being, and I have to admit, I still do.

If we had a dog, that dog would have bitten that nasty woman. I watched her in horror as she chased a neighbour's dog out of our yard with a baseball bat. Anyone who doesn't have compassion for animals is deeply troubled. This was a red flag that my father ignored. He ignored many because he thought that he needed a wife for his three little girls.

Many years later when I was visiting him and his wife was in the kitchen, he leaned over to me and said, "I guess if I hadn't remarried we would have done just fine." To which I replied, "Yes, I have to agree, I know we would have been more than fine." I was shocked that he was making this admission to me at this late stage in life. I took it as his way of apologizing because, clearly, he got it wrong.

It is because of her that I live with Complex Post Traumatic Stress Disorder. She is a red flag. I feel for any child that had her as a teacher or choir director at church. I am sure that she abused other children too. Her temper was so explosive that she could not control it. There is something very wrong with her to this day. Now that my dad has passed on, I don't have to bother with her anymore, and that is the best part of my life.

Key Takeaway - The Lesson

Early childhood trauma changes our brain. The way to heal it is in nature with animals. Neurofeedback and hypnosis are also great ways to heal the brain. It can be healed. I am proof of this, but it takes time and energy to be quiet in nature with animals. This is why I created Healing Minis Farm School, so that there is a place to do just this.

If a person sparks something in you, spend as much time with them as you can to determine whether they are real or fake. People can fake it for months, even years, but everyone shows their true colours eventually. Wait for when there is a challenging and stressful situation and pay attention to how they react. Working with a partner is a great way to see how they operate. Mine just ordered me around and micromanaged and complained about everything that I did. My step-mother was the same, and I often would call my husband by her name as I could see the similarity in their disorders.

Dogs are the way to start healing. There are so many unwanted dogs - go get one. Make sure that you can afford to feed them and pay the vet bill of course, but they are well worth every penny. They give way more than we ever could, and we are the ones who benefit the most from having them in our lives. Be ready, willing and able to jump at the opportunities that come upon your path just like your dog is always ready and willing to go anywhere with you.

Chapter 16:
Learn to Let Go

This is probably the hardest part of being a parent and a dog owner. Knowing when to hold them close and when to let them go. Sensing when it is time for us to "put the dog down".I had to put Babe and Chloe down, and it was the hardest thing I ever had to do! I sure hope I don't ever have to make that decision again.

As parents, there comes a time in all of our lives when we have to let our children go Whether it is their first day of school or the first day of college, we can't hold onto them forever. Even though some children never leave home, these cases are rare. Adult children are moving back home with their parents, and this is becoming more and more of the norm these days. Many adult children who cannot find jobs return to the home of their parents just to survive. Housing costs have skyrocketed while buying groceries is almost impossible.

In February of 2016, Babe started limping and her hind legs started to give out. I let her off of the leash so that I could help her get up better, and since she was walking so slowly, I knew she couldn't get away from me. This went on for a few days but one day, she got away from me and dashed down toward the frozen creek.

I spent the entire day looking for her. I fell through the ice trying to find her and had to run home and get out of my freezing clothes before hypothermia set in. I posted it on social media and a wonderful boy went down on the creek on his skidoo and rescued her. It seems she couldn't get up and was just lying there. When I went to his house to pick her up, she was lying on a sled in his garage and she couldn't walk. He helped me to lift her into the car, and then we started using a strap to help her lift her hind end. I took her to the animal hospital.

The vet, a woman, brought up euthanasia and I was infuriated. I wasn't ready to let her go, and I was so angry that this vet had the nerve to even bring it up. When I told her that I didn't believe in that she snarled back, "Well maybe you will when she is sitting in her own pee and poo." I wanted to leave that vet right then and there and never come back. They tried to woo me back saying that it was just a "personality conflict" and that they would make sure that I would never have to deal with that vet again.

I started giving her a drop of Rick Simpson cannabis oil every day, and Babe got better and started walking normally again. I realized that the Creator had answered my prayers and gave me a little more time with her. I spent that spring and summer doting over her, and finally on September 3, 2016, the vet came to our home and euthanized her, something I thought I would never do. In the end she was right. I did know when she was lying in her own excrement that she wanted to go, but that was seven months later. I feel so blessed to have had the privilege of walking with this dog through the last few years of her life. She is buried along with Kodi and Shamus in the Forget Me Not Garden. My little cemetery is growing, and I have decided that I want my ashes buried with them. That is what they do in Jamaica. They dig a hole in their backyard and bury their loved one right there on their property where they are always close by. I think that is a beautiful thing but highly illegal in North America, so this idea of planting ashes with a tree really appeals to me.

I have let go of religious dogma and lies. I walked away from a lifetime of religion. Dogs don't need religion because they are already god-like. They love us unconditionally, they are always there for us, they are excited to see us and always enthusiastic, they comfort us when we are sad and protect us. Doesn't that sound like a higher power to you?

I have learned to let go of the false expectations that I have for people as they almost always let me down. My own family haven't been very supportive, and unfortunately there have been some very mean-spirited campaigns by some of them to discredit me. I have let every single person who tried to bring me down go. Life truly is too short to worry about people who are not able to love you. Move on, there are plenty who will love you, so stop wasting your time with the ones who are simply unable to.

Letting go can be so freeing yet difficult to do. When I finally let go of my dogs, it was excruciatingly difficult. But love knows no bounds, and I could clearly see that they were suffering. Let go of the pain others have caused you so that you are not full of anger, bitterness and rage. Letting go is a form of self-love and that is something that I am finally learning to do. Letting go and learning to love myself are my big lessons. Dogs don't need to learn these lessons because they already know how to let go and love themselves.

Let go of unrealistic expectations that you place upon yourself. You don't have to get married; you don't have to have children. You can travel the world if you want and have various lovers. You don't have to be with the same person for 50 years. That is wonderful if you want to be, but so many of those marriages are not happy ones - they are enduring ones. A woman in the 1070s couldn't have a credit card or get a mortgage without a man. There was little choice for our grandmothers.

Dogs endure for us, but we get rid of them every chance that we get. As I type this, shelters are full with unwanted dogs and cats. I am just now, at age 60, embarking on the creative pursuits that I have wanted my entire life. Things like writing, producing, creating music and working with other creatively minded people are what bring joy to my life, that and dogs.

Key Takeaway - The Lesson

Don't water down your life just to make other people happy. If your friends scoff at your dreams, get better friends and keep dreaming. Life is indeed what you make it, and people who sit around and complain all day end up sick and miserable. Believe me, I know. I have lived with many of them, and finally I am very happy to be living, alone, with my dogs (because yes, Lola needed a few friends) and my horses. Never, ever shall my security, my safe haven, be threatened, by a man or anyone else for that matter. Always keep a dog close. They are the best predictor of a good human being.

Chapter 17:
Never Judge a Book by Its Cover

When I met Kodi, at her owner's home in rural eastern Ontario, she was a mess. Her beautiful mane was greasy, and to pet her left your hand full of the oil. To judge her outward appearance, most wouldn't want to be near her much less touch her, as she was dirty, disheveled and a bit depressed, like her owner and master, Artie. I thought she was beautiful and she followed me wherever I went. Her tail wagged as I looked into her eyes, and I promised her that I would bring her home with me one day. Why I told this massive creature this, I don't know. I just knew that she was going to be living with me on the six acres with a river had miraculously purchased only six months earlier. It became our place of peace and tranquility.

Artie told me that this place wasn't good for his mental health. I stayed close to him until he was ready to pick up the brokenness of his past and Ready to Love Me ("Ready to Love You" is a song by Brian Adams, the song we chose to walk down the aisle to at our wedding a few years later).

He missed his two daughters and felt controlled and manipulated by their mother who used them to get what she wanted out of him, namely, his money. He could never say no to her, even though he would thoroughly interrogate her about the use of the thousands upon thousands of dollars he had given her. In the end, he always gave in. I can understand this as I lived the same life only hundreds of miles away in London, Ontario.

It was easier not to react to my then husband's barrage of lies and profanities, name calling, belittling of me and my family, raging uncontrollably, turning red in the face and no longer in control of his faculties. It is easier to give in and try to give them what they wanted (Artie's ex wanted money and things; mine just wanted to be waited on and fed). There is a name for it, codependency, and we both became dependent on taking care of our then significant other. I will never forget the moment, after nearly 10 years of marriage, when the light bulb finally went on.

I was standing in the kitchen and my then husband was ranting and raving - his usual raging behaviour that I had learned to live with. Our youngest daughter was hiding under the kitchen table and God told me to look at her face. I did, and all I saw was terror. It was like everything else in the room dimmed and the spotlight was on her. I couldn't even hear what he was screaming anymore. I only saw her terrified face looking at me. My eldest daughter heard the commotion and ran out to see what was wrong. Upon seeing her younger sister distraught and crying, she tried to console her while she looked at me. In that instant I heard God say, "Look at their faces." I looked.

I will never forget the look on their faces. It broke my heart. God clearly told me: "YOU are doing this to them by staying here, by staying in this marriage. It is time to go." I ushered them up the stairs to safety and told my then husband that he was not to come upstairs. I did the only thing I knew to do: I prayed, and a few days later, I called my dad to tell him I was getting a divorce.

Within three short months, I had found a job, purchased a house, secured a line of credit and gotten my soon to be ex-husband a mortgage, so that he could keep the house. I had to take on all of the debt from the marriage but it was worth it. The day we left was one of the happiest of my life.

On the closing date, he instructed his lawyer to give me only half of what we had agreed on, leaving me several thousand dollars short for my down payment. The woman at the bank, after hearing about my dilemma said, "Aren't you getting a 5% cash back on this mortgage? Well, we will just use that. It is half a dozen of one and six of another." I couldn't believe it as I had been told that I could not use the 5% cash back toward my down payment, but here I was, doing just that. Only God can move heaven and Earth to get you out of your latest circumstance, and when

He/She does, it is another lesson in life. Learning to depend on your own internal light and no one else is a lesson we all need to learn and quickly! The divine source of love has never let me down, and I don't imagine that it ever will.

I knew that Kodi was lonely. I could see it in her eyes, for her master traveled for his work and was gone for weeks on end, working in the mines in remote places. Places like Indonesia, Greenland and the Northwest Territories. When his ex (and the mother of his two daughters) left him and sued him for child and spousal support, he started working abroad.

That year I found freedom from the slavery I had been living in. Not just in my marriage, but also in my Church. The "pastors" decided to lie and told members of the church that I was an adulterer, in a "bad place" and to stay away from me. That was absolutely not true, but it was reported to me by several members of the "church." This church has many things wrong with it, not just what they did to me, but what they have done and continue to do to others.

A pastor is not a trained counsellor. When a pastor tells people how and what they should believe "or else" they will be shunned, it is called abuse, not spiritual counselling. Dogs protect us from potential harm and comfort us when someone has been abusive to us. They are the healing balm from the negative and abusive people in our lives.

I was raised as a minister's daughter so I did believe in marriage at one point. Artie never wanted to marry previously, so I don't know why he chose to marry me. I was planning a trip with my daughters, since he was usually gone at Christmas, and it turned out that he was going to be home after all. I was looking at Jamaica, and he said, "Do you want to get married in Jamaica?" to which I said, "Yes."

On New Year's day, with our four daughters in tow, we got married in Montego Bay, Jamaica. Marriage is the best of two people forging ahead together and, despite the tribulation and hardship, choosing to love each other. The problem is most people don't even know how to love themselves, let alone anyone else. Marriage, as I mentioned previously, is more to the benefit of the male. The marriage union comes with each other's baggage. I hadn't gotten over my first marriage when I met my second husband. I was broken and so was he. He found me on a chat line, and his kindness and creativity drew me in. There were signs that I ignored, but I was committed to becoming the best step-mother ever.

Blending a family is never an easy task. I came with two daughters and so did he. One of them started acting out the moment we walked into the airport and didn't stop until the day after our wedding, when the truth came tumbling out. My step-daughter confided in me, and I was honoured that she trusted me enough to tell me her darkest secrets. I only wish that I had the power to make things better for her. I had a natural instinct to want to love and protect her, to rescue her from the horror she was describing. I have learned that, even though I tried to rescue her from her miserable life, the only person I can truly rescue is myself. I have since given up the rescuing gig. It doesn't pay well and always leaves me with a bitter taste in my mouth. I will stick to rescuing dogs and horses.

Kodi never had to be on a leash or tied up again once she got to my home. She wouldn't wander off the property. She would stay close by, ready to pounce on any negative force that would find its way to our door, and she would chase it away, protecting her family.

She didn't cause me a moment of grief and was always there and waiting to be loved. I was so happy that she had the freedom to roam, and even though I would bring her in on really cold days, the truth was she was a snow dog and could be seen sitting out in the middle of a snow storm, covered in white snow, her black face peering out. Always watchful, always protecting her home and her family.

Key Takeaway - The Lesson

Learn to be open, allowing opportunities to come and go. People may look scary but are really lovely on the inside. Dogs don't judge our appearance and aren't concerned with it, quite frankly. We spend billions of dollars every year in North America on beauty products, clothes, purses, shoes, etc. What a colossal waste of money, especially when there are Indigenous people who don't have clean drinking water in Canada. We care more about our outward appearance than our integrity and character, and it's a real shame. All of us are going to get old and fall apart one day, and yes, die. Imagine if we took that money to feed the world and put a stop to war and famine once and for all. Never judge another person or animal by the way they look or even by the way they act. Many dogs have been abused and need healing, which only love can do.

Chapter 18:
Be Afraid of the Thunder

Kodi hated thunder, but you could find her lying out in the worst snowstorm. She would be a big snowball, with her brown eyes staring out at the world. This massive dog would cower in fear when it thundered. She would try to get into my bed to be as close as possible to me when the thunder came. I would console her and tell her it was alright and that she had nothing to be afraid of, but she still cowered. She was afraid of thunder and loud noises. So am I.

My second husband found her living in a culvert under a road, and she was afraid of him. It took him three days of bringing her food before she trusted him enough to go home with him. She had just had a litter of pups and was very fearful of humans. He rescued her at the insistence of his young daughter and cared for her until the day that I met her. I even cooked for her. She was the queen who never disappointed me.

We should be afraid of the thunder of other people and their unresolved anger issues. I spent my childhood trying to avoid that thunder of my step-mother (out of control rage) and then 10 years with my now ex-husband, which was like walking on eggshells, never knowing when the next explosion would erupt. They leave destruction in their path and the innocent bystanders (wife, children and pets) are the first casualties in domestic violence. If I had a dog like Kodi back then, she would not have liked the loud thunderous voice of my ex-husband, ridiculing me and my faith every chance he got.

He was a tyrant and a verbal abuser and Kodi would never have put up with that, but I did, for 10 years. Until the universe said move, and I did, to the other side of the province where I could find peace, tranquility and happiness and never put up with abuse of any kind especially from someone who vowed to love me. Little did I know that I would just repeat the same unhealthy attachments with a narcissistic type man. Emotionally unavailable like my dad with a need to criticize and always be right like my step-parent. Throw in perfectionism and OCD and it's the perfect storm for more trauma.

I love flowers of all kinds. I think it is because I spent so much time outside as a child that the flowers and small creatures became my friends. I was never lonely and I never wanted to go inside. I was happiest playing outside. The little library a block from my house was my place of refuge and is why it is so important to continue supporting our local libraries.

One year, when my daughter was only three, I was leaving to take her for a little walk to the corner store. I was suspicious when I saw my then husband working in the front walkway garden of wild flowers. He rarely helped at all so to see him weeding a garden, all bent over, made me suspicious.I was wondering what he was up to. I was very proud of these gorgeous flowers. They grew tall, in brilliant colours, and they were a mess. Not orderly and neat but rather wild, full of colour and excitement. I wanted to plant them everywhere, but my first husband argued with me. He didn't like them. He said they made our house look like a dump with weeds everywhere.

I stood there like a deer in the headlights; how could anyone think that these flowers were anything but beautiful? I knew when I saw him working in the garden, something he never did, that he was up to no good. I told him not to pull the flowers out by the root or they won't grow back, to please just cut them back. They will be even more beautiful next year.

I don't know why I was surprised, but I was. When I came back only a few minutes later, there were my beloved wildflowers, every one of them, pulled out by the root, not a single one left. I was stunned as he looked at me with a smirk on his face. I remember thinking, "Wow, you sure must hate me to do such a mean and spiteful thing to me, to destroy something that I loved." I had hoped some would come back the next year, but they never did. It took another seven years before I left. I had experienced this once before in an abusive relationship when I was a teenager.

It was with an older man who would destroy my clothes, my jewelry, my purse, whatever he thought would hurt me the most, and this was the same thing and the same feeling of utter sadness.

It was 1981. I was barely 18 and it took me a while to see the glaring truth that this man was not for me. He was a friend of my sister's boyfriend, another drug dealer, abuser. He had me carry his stash of drugs for him. I am sweet and innocent looking and no one would suspect that I am carrying a pound of hash or cocaine in my bag.

He attacked me on busy streets, biting my face after a dinner at a nice restaurant in downtown Ottawa because one of the other diners we were with, a male, had made conversation with me, and he was insanely jealous. I had blood running down my face as I fled down the busy street waving at cars to stop and help me. One, filled with men, stopped, but when they saw the blood on my face and the guy in pursuit, they slammed the door in my face and sped off. Even the bus driver was oblivious to the fact that my abuser was now sitting beside me on the last bus home for the night, a bus that stopped 15 kms away from my home. He sat beside me, and when the blood pouring down my face bothered him, he grabbed my face and licked the blood off.

I got off the bus at the last possible stop. Why I didn't ask the bus driver for help, I will never know. He grabbed my bag and threw it as hard as he could into the open field. I knew he was crazy for sure because he just threw away a kilo of hashish that he had stashed in my bag, along with my textbooks from college. I ran into the street and flagged down another car, and this time, it was an elderly couple, who wanted to take me to the hospital, but I insisted that I just wanted to go home. Of course, I didn't go home, I went instead to a close friend Dustin's house and he and his sister took care of me (they wanted me to go to the hospital too, but again I refused). I was afraid of all of the questions they would have at the hospital. In retrospect, I should have gone. Perhaps I wouldn't carry this scar on my face, or maybe this whole ordeal would have ended earlier.

When I arrived home the next day with a huge gash and bruise on my face, my father asked me how it had happened. Of course, I lied and said that I had hit it on the corner of a car door. "I've heard that before," he responded, but that was it. It wasn't until this same man stalked me in my neighbourhood and attacked me, disrupting my parents' Bible study, that they realized how much trouble I had gotten myself into. How can I love someone like this? I can't, and I had stopped caring about him long before, but as a stalker, he would not stop following me, which is why I fled to London, Ontario, the place of my father's birth and where his sister (my dear Auntie Em, who took us in when we were young) and my older cousin lived.

Little did I know that I was going from the fire into the frying pan by living with my older cousin, who also partied a bit too much, had a bad temper and had lots of company at all hours of the night. Within a few months, after he had raped me and then kicked me out, my sweet Auntie Em came to my rescue and took me in and helped me to find another place close to the university where I was a student.

I stayed in my marriage seven years before I realized that I was living in an abusive relationship, and even then, it did not cross my mind to leave him. I played the part of the dutiful wife, working full-time, taking care of all of the girls' needs, cleaning, cooking, shopping and even doing the outside work. If something broke down, I had to rely on the kindness of male friends or pay a professional because my husband had no interest in anything but the television.

Consequently, the same time I met my first husband, I was diagnosed with Post Traumatic Stress Disorder, the result of a car accident. One in which I was simply stopped in the road, waiting to turn left, when an Italian woman, who spoke no English and was yelling at her unruly children, slammed into me at 60 mph. The psychologist who diagnosed me said that the car accident was like a gateway to the past. Because my mother died in a car accident when I was a baby, this accident opened the floodgates of long buried memories of molestation and utter betrayal. One of the symptoms of this disorder is being easily scared.

I knew when the storm was coming. I knew it with my step-mother, I knew it with that abusive boyfriend, and I knew it then with my ex-husband. The quiet before the storm, the dark brooding, the silent stares, the constant demeaning and hurtful comments meant to hurt you. When people are hurt, they either strike out at others or internalize it and strike out at themselves, such as in the case of substance abuse. My ex-husband did both.

I tried for 10 years to encourage him to do something with his life, go back to school or go to therapy for the many years he lived as a drug addict and alcoholic, to no avail. It was a wonder I survived all those years. If not for my children, I would never have stayed that long. Now I realize that it isn't in the best interests of the children to ever stay in an abusive relationship. I thought that because he didn't hit, kick or bite me, like the previous abuser did, then it wasn't abuse, but it was and we need to start calling it what it is instead of dancing around this horrible bad habit people have fallen into.

Education is the key, and there needs to be a lot more about domestic violence. If you have to beat someone to stay with you (either physically or verbally), then it doesn't say much about you, does it? Domestic violence isn't just about beating with your fists;it is also about beating with your words, your money and your controlling mood.

During those long 10 years, God never left me, andthe universe never did forsake me. Even though I cried myself to sleep more times than I can remember, He/She heard my cries and He/She dried my tears. He/She showed me the way by guiding me to go back to school and get my Masters of Social Work so that I could escape from the hell I was living in called marriage.

When God told me it was time to leave (and He/She did), everything just fell into place. I found a job, a house, a bank who would work with me, even though I had a bankruptcy from the past, and best of all, it was far, far, far away from him. And the icing on the cake, the six acres that I bought with a river running through it has wildflowers everywhere! The creator gave me back what my ex-husband tried to steal from me, and he did it overflowing because everywhere I look, there is always a new flower forming. Even though I thought I would lose this place, during my meditation I always heard, "You are not going to lose what God has given to you."

Now Lola and I live on our six acres and love taking walks down the trail to the South Nation River. She growled at a man yesterday and even scared me. This man isn't very nice to his wife, I have noticed, and Lola seems to agree. She is fine with his wife but goes nuts whenever he comes around. If I had a dog like Lola when I was with my first husband, she surely would have stopped him from being abusive. She always would stand in front of me when my now husband became verbally abusive. He knew better than to try to physically hurt me because she would have bitten him. We are both so glad that he is finally gone from our lives, and I have worked very hard to be able to decipher whether a person is authentic or just acting, like so many people do.

If you are living with an abusive person, there is a way out. It might take some time and some planning and help from trusted family and friends, but please, don't stay. You are only given one life to live, and living it to try to please an abusive person is just a waste of your time and energy. Take it from me - know when it is time to leave and never, ever look back.

Key Takeaway - The Lesson

If your dog consistently shows aggression toward a person, be very wary of that person. Dogs and horses do not lie. They pick up on the energy of each one of us. Some are very protective and will bark at everyone, like my dog, Lola, does, but she calms down once she knows they are not a threat. She lets people know that she is in charge and so should we. So many of us who are survivors, unfortunately, also become doormats because we don't know any better. We become accustomed to being treated poorly that we barely recognize it. Pay attention to your dog and your intuition because neither will ever lead you in the wrong direction.

Chapter 19:
Sticks and Stones May Break My Bones But Names Will Never Hurt Me

Words, spoken in anger and in rage hurt just as much (and sometimes more) as being hit or kicked, especially when they are said by someone who says they love you. The external wounds from a beating heal in time, but the emotional and verbal abuse stays with you for decades and sometimes for a lifetime. My dogs have never found fault in me, even though there are many, and they truly accept me the way I am, no question. How many people do you know who you can say the same thing about?

My step-mother as I mentioned, is a perfectionist so I have grown up in her unrealistic world, in which she suffers from migraine headaches. My ex-husband would try to say the most hateful things to me to cause me pain when he was in one of his emotional rages. My eldest daughter's father was void of emotions or feelings and cared only about fishing and hunting. My present husband, from whom I am estranged, calls me horrible names when he is frustrated that he can't control me anymore. Heck, he even threatened to shoot me in the head and has been charged with uttering death threats and assault. I even found the gun and the bullets, and he isn't a hunter. Thank God for restraining orders. Without them, I wouldn't be living the free and happy life that I am.

Words can hurt, more than a punch. Emotional pain is poison, and we spread it amongst ourselves. I have to admit, being of both Irish (known for their quick temper and love of the bottle) and Scottish (also known for their quick temper and love of the bottle) descent when I am fired up, like a mother lion who would die protecting her cubs, watch out. I am unstoppable, and sometimes that's not such a good thing.

I was diagnosed in 1993 with Post Traumatic Stress Disorder, which at the time, I barely had heard of, but when I studied the symptoms, "easily frightened, jumpy, problems with sleep and mood either depression, anxiety or both it all made perfect sense. Vivid flashbacks of a trauma for me stemmed from infancy with the death of my mother, throughout my childhood of incest (maternal grandfather), drug and alcohol abuse in my teenage years resulting in rape and assault as well as severely acting out in extremely harmful ways.

I remember those days, even though they are more than 30 years ago, I will never forget the domestic violence I experienced with an older man when I was barely 18. It is the reason why I left Ottawa to live in London, because, when I tried to get away from this guy, he followed me. He even became a cabbie so that he could follow me around all day. He was obsessed beyond belief and very violent. I will never forget the first time I was attacked by a man who was supposed to be my "boyfriend".

He was living with a few other men and had to go out to get some more dope and told me to wait for him in his room. I decided to have a nap, but with strange men in the house, I slipped under the covers with my clothes intact. Hours later, when he returned, he saw that I was fully clothed and immediately became suspicious. In his twisted mind he was sure that I had had sexual relations with one of his roommates, or why else would I be fully clothed in bed? He threw me from one side of the room to the other as I screamed out in horror. Not one of those men, who were downstairs at the time, came to my aide. His face was red with rage as he grabbed onto my Levi's and totally ripped them off my body. I was shocked beyond belief and did not understand what was going on.

When he finally calmed down, I had nothing to wear, and I couldn't even escape if I wanted to because I had no pants and there was no way I was going out in public without any pants on. He had found a way to make me stay, apologizing over and over and over again. I had to stay the night, and the next day, he went to a thrift shop and got me a pair of jeans, which were a size too small but I managed to squeeze them on and make the long bus ride home. Why I ever returned to this guy, I will never know. Of course he wined and dined me to prove his sincerity and I felt sorry for him, and thought, mistakenly, that I could somehow help him. What a naïve girl I was and still am sometimes!

I had started to attend Algonquin College in General Arts and Sciences in Ottawa because who knows what they want to be when they are 18? I met some fabulous women; two were sisters, very French and great fun to be around, Gina and Nina. Another was a quiet girl named Anna. We all became close friends, and I spent many nights crashing on Gina's couch after a night of partying at the pub.

We were all in the same classes, and one, Human Relations, opened my eyes to the cyclical nature of abuse. I still have the textbook by Ronald Adler called "Looking Out, Looking In" and started using it in the Communications classes I taught at the local community college, near where I live. Talk about a full circle. I always wanted to teach this kind of material, and now, decades later, here I am, doing just that. The General Arts and Sciences Program gave me the confidence to register for university as it was the first time in my life that I got straight As. This guy tried to interfere with that, and he was vicious and became my stalker when I tried to break up with him on multiple occasions.

He would wait outside of my classroom and when I would try to ignore him. He broke into my locker and took my winter coat, forcing me to have to speak to him. Gina and Nina were tough girls, and they went right up to him and snatched my coat from him and told him off. I was never so proud in my life with my newfound friends! French girls can be very tough, much tougher than me! For the first time in my life, someone stood up for ME!

He continued to follow us, trying to intimidate my friends, but they protected me like no one ever had or has since, in my life. He attacked me one night on the street corner. I was with Anna, and he had thrown me up against a glass window and spat in my face. Anna grabbed me by the hand and yelled "run," and we ran, for blocks and blocks and blocks, until we couldn't run anymore. We went back to her apartment, and I spent the night and went home the next day. I don't know why it hadn't occurred to me before to run, but it didn't. I had no idea about the responses to trauma; freeze, fight, flight, fawn.

This relationship ended in the courtroom when a restraining order was placed upon him with a stiff fine and probation for attacking me in my neighbourhood. But he didn't stay away from me; he continued to stalk me. That is the reason why I left and went so far away to London. I didn't think that he would go that far to find me, and I was right. I have heard that he has children and that he has been in and out of jail for most of his life. Those poor children. I learned to forgive him too. I had to, or else I would carry the scars forever.

In 2015, I was spending the weekend at a spa with an old friend celebrating our birthdays. During dinner she asked me if I remembered the night that I showed up at her house and was covered in bruises and had said that I had been raped by this same "boyfriend." I was stunned because I didn't remember that night, and I still don't. I was raped and I don't even remember it. How can that be? Now I realize it is fine that I don't remember. Who would want to remember that? A few years later, I ended that "friendship" for good. I noticed how she supported all of our mutual male friends' careers, but she never supported mine. Why on Earth would anyone bring up such a traumatic event from the past when we are trying to have a nice dinner? I couldn't wait to get away from her after that. I closed right up, and any trust I did have was shattered.

Dogs can't talk and hurt each other with their thoughts and words. All of my dogs have accepted me just as I am, loved me regardless and were always so happy to see me, no matter what. They all truly love me and I them.

If only we could learn to love each other this way. Life would be a little better, a little lighter, a little easier to live if we truly felt loved unconditionally, the way that dogs love us. The first thing we need to do is to learn to love ourselves. We have all heard it before, that you can't love others until you love yourself. I never really believed it as I always thought love was about sacrifice.

I watched my dad sacrifice time after time after time just to keep the peace with my step-mother, his wife. Look to your pets to see what true love is all about. You will find it there.

Sometimes angels come in unexpected forms like a dog, or a street person. Having dogs around me makes me feel safe and secure as I know their loyalty truer than anyone else in my life. Sometimes when people have disappointed you to the point that you no longer have any trust left, animals are the way back to learning how to trust again.

Key Takeaway - The Lesson

Domestic violence isn't always about violence. Sometimes, it is quiet gaslighting, "You're crazy," or subtle digs "That chocolate bar has 1000 calories". When you grow up being hit, shamed, neglected and abused, you end up in the same type of relationships over and over and over again until you finally get it. I finally got it. But it took more than 50 years, so don't you wait that long to find your freedom in this world.

Many women stay in abusive relationships simply because of a lack of finances. It is imperative for all women to have a means to support themselves so they don't have to depend on anyone else. Several different income streams are optimal. The power of the internet has made becoming extremely wealthy within reach for many of us entrepreneurs. Use what you make to give back to the world. Help women who are trying to leave abusive men by donating to women's shelters or to a charity that helps vulnerable women, whether it is here in Canada or in Congo - just do it.

Sponsor a child and start writing letters back and forth for a lasting legacy of how one person can change another person's life, dramatically and positively. Don't allow yourself to be blind to the red flags that surround you. Pay attention to the subtle signals that your angels and guides are trying to show you. You are never alone, even if it feels like it sometimes. Everyone can benefit from having a dog in their lives.

Chapter 20:
Play Like My Puppies - Ethel and Lucy

If we could capture the enthusiasm of a dog when they have the zoomies, we would get a lot more done. You know when they get a sudden burst of energy and they run like mad all over the place? They have built up energy that needs to be spent, and so they do. This is an act of play. Dogs are the best at playing. They don't need any toys; they will play with a stick, a rock or even their own tail. Throw a ball and they will undoubtedly chase it. Dogs never forget how to play. Even when they get older, they maintain an aspect of playfulness.

When Lola turned three years old, I saw two Bernese/hound dog mixed female puppies for sale and just knew they would be perfect for Lola and me. On August 9, 2024, these two-month-old beauties came home to live with us at Healing Minis Farm School, and the timing, as always, was just right. I am living alone, as my daughter moved out with her boyfriend, and I have the time it takes to train two sweet puppies. They are extremely affectionate and give me my daily dose of endorphins through their cuddling and love.

These two play all day long, and they play hard. Then they have a nap, a snack and drink and start all over again. Their lives are blissfully sweet, and I am so thrilled to be sharing it with them. They are my comfort in the middle of the night. They know just when I need a cuddle and have no problem climbing up onto my lap and resting their sweet little head upon my shoulder. Is there anything that feels better than that?

When people age, they laugh less and don't play much at all. Children laugh 300 times a day whereas the average adult over 40 laughs four times a day. Some adults play too much, like when a person can't tear themselves away from the TV, or computer, or golf course or whatever it is that they can't get enough of. It becomes an addiction. My dad was addicted to watching sports, like so many people are. I, on the other hand, never watch sports. I find it boring and a complete waste of time, yes, even hockey! Our dogs don't care about watching sports; they would rather be playing sports with us.

The amount of money spent on sporting events is mind blowing. With children starving throughout the world, we pay a football player, a basketball player, a hockey player millions upon millions of dollars just to watch them play. Don't get me wrong, I love playing sports, but watching them, no thanks.

Dogs are the same way: they want to play, not sit around and watch us play. They are interactive like that. I don't fit in with this world, I know that much, but sporting events also draw out sex trafficking, and during the huge events, sexual assault and trafficking sky rocket. Think about that next time you go to spend hundreds of dollars at a sporting event. What do people do as they are watching sports? They drink beer and wine and lots of it. Dogs have no need for these substances. They just want to play.

We spend our lives working, being gone for eight hours a day for five days while our dogs stay at home and wait for us. Some might be lucky enough to spend their days at a doggie day care, but that gets expensive at $35.00 per day. When we come home, both our dogs and kids just want to play with us. We have to get the kids and the animals fed, clean the house, walk the dog, feed the dog, clean up the poop and on and on and on it goes. My point is, take the time to play with your dog and your kids. One day they will be gone from your life and you will be missing these important moments when you decided to play instead of work.

We have lost our sense of play. Sports isn't playing. Sports is competing, and there is a huge difference. We chase a ball around a huge area, trying to get it into a net, and whoever has the most points in the end wins. There is always a winner and always a loser. There is no way around it. But playing and being carefree is so much better.

Playing with your dog, at the end of a day, helps to relieve the stress from the day. Playing with your dog also strengthens the bond you have with them. It gives you both the opportunity to expand some built up energy and get some exercise, which we know is the best thing for depression. Play is really important. Life isn't just about work and money. Play releases endorphins, the body's natural pain killer, which improves mood and mental health.

Play with your dog. Play with your kids. Play with your partner. Get out there and play. Find something that you love to do whether it is pickleball or art class and bring someone with you. It doesn't only help with your relationship with your dog, but it does the same thing for people too. Research has found that laughter and play are key ingredients in having a happy and blanched relationship. Play is even good for our brains because it helps to reduce stress, improve relationships and provide physical health. It is imperative for adults to learn how to incorporate play into their lives, and having a dog to play with, is one of the easiest and best ways to do that.

We have lost our way in this world because we need more and more and more. We need a better job, car, house, vacation, clothes, jewelry - it just never ends. We spend our lives working and toiling to take care of ourselves and others, but in the process, we burn out because we stopped playing. We stopped having fun. Dogs bring the fun back, so go out to a rescue and adopt one. You won't be sorry.

Key Takeaway - The Lesson

Everyone needs a hobby. Not just any hobby, a hobby that you are passionate about. Learning to have fun as an adult can be a daunting task. I find spending time with young people and animals does the trick, but so does volunteering. I am so happy that I volunteer for The Ottawa Grassroots Festival and Roots Canada as a music journalist. I have met Juno award winning artists and call these celebrated musicians my friends. Music and writing are my passions, so anything that has to do with those two things brings me great joy. Everyone has something they love to do or are gifted at. Playing with your children, grandchildren and pets are natural ways to instill a sense of wonder and reduce stress. Happiness is an internal job, and it is up to each one of us to find our own, so that we can share it with others.

Becoming a philanthropist is a high calling and one that I adore. There is nothing better than being able to give to others so that their lives can be improved. I have always sponsored girls from Africa and am now working to bring my adult sponsor daughters from Ethiopia to North Augusta. I am opening an African Restaurant so that they have a job when they get here and am renovating my home into two apartments so that they have a safe and affordable place to live. I have even signed up to take a graduate certificate in immigration and citizenship from Queen's University in Kingston, Ontario, in the new year so that I can help not only them, but others who are trying to escape the horrors of war. I encourage you to stay in touch and check in with me on social media to find ways that you can give back because I am always looking for great employees and volunteers.

Conclusion

It is my hope, for anyone who has survived childhood trauma, to find healing, in the most simplest of ways, by spending time with their dog. I know that they teach us incredible lessons like learning to wait, being faithful and showing our loved ones how happy we are to see them again. They are always excited and willing to go with us wherever we want, no questions asked. There is just no better friend than a dog.

Despite the many difficulties and obstacles that we face in life, we can find healing through a dog, and it is my sincere hope that anyone who reads this book who doesn't have a dog will get one and realize the immense emotional support that they provide to improve our mental health. Stay far away from people who don't like dogs.

My dogs have taught me how to love. They show me when I need to sit and be quiet and when it is ok to show my exorbitant love. They never hurt me or ignore me. They truly want the best for all of us. Most of all, they teach me how to remain in the now, the present moment, which is all we really have. It is in the present moments where there is peace and life is so much sweeter. Disease comes from stress, so having a dog is one of life's greatest stress relievers. If you already have a dog in your family, you already know this. Know that you can heal from all of life's traumas - you just need to get yourself a dog.

"Emancipate yourselves from mental slavery-
none but ourselves can free our minds."

Bob Marley

Meet Laurie Bowen, B.Ed., C.D.C, M.S.W.

Laurie Lynn Bowen, is an author and freelance music journalist, who, after spending two decades as a Social Worker, knew that she needed more music in her life. She interned with The Ottawa Grassroots Festival while studying Scriptwriting at Algonquin College in Ottawa in 2021/22, and has never looked back. She found her tribe in this group of music enthusiasts.

Laurie teaches Mental Health and Addictions, English, Horse Powered Reading, Stress Management, Laughter Yoga, Meditation, Dance For Parkinson's and Other Motion Disorders, Montessori Methods for Alzheimer's and Dementia, Forest Bathing, Equine Assisted

Learning and Personal Coaching, at Healing Minis Farm School, in North Augusta, Ontario. It is a place where you can get back in touch with nature by spending time with three miniature horses who are sisters, Ruby, Oppie and Emmie. (www.healingminisfarmschool.com)

Laurie is a Registered Dramatic Arts Teacher, Scriptwriter, Director, Producer, Actor, Singer, Motivational Speaker and Owner of Arts For Life Productions. www.artsforlifeproductions.com

She has written the script and lyrics for Send Me An Angel The Musical and is getting ready to record the soundtrack. Life Lessons I Learned From My Dogs is her first book.

Laurie is a fierce advocate for women's well-being and is dedicated to empowering Congolese Women to take control of their lives through entrepreneurial endeavors and volunteers with Friends of The Congo www.friendsofthecongo.org

She is an advocate for www.fradaameck.com , a Congolese company that is helping to feed the displaced people in the conflict area.

Laurie is happily living life on her little farm, with her horses and dogs.

A grandmother, a mother, an auntie, a sister and a dear friend to many, who have come upon her enlightened path.

- Instagram: @laurielynn_bowen
- Facebook:@laurielynn
- LinkedIn: Laurie Bowen
- Tiktok: @lauriebowen1
- Email: healingminis@gmail.com and laurielynnbowen@yahoo.ca
- www.artsforlifeproductions.com
- www.healingminisfarmschool.ca

thank you

Thank you for reading my book!

Dear Reader,

Well, you made it to the end—congrats! I hope you found some insights, and maybe even a bit of inspiration along the way. Sharing these stories and lessons has been a real adventure, and I'm thrilled you chose to spend your time with me.

Now, I need your help!

If you found value in these pages (or if you just really like dogs and success stories), I'd love it if you could take a minute to leave a 5-star review on Amazon and Shoply. Not only will it make my day, but it'll also help this book reach more people who could benefit from it. Think of it as a little ripple effect—your review could be the nudge someone needs to pick up the book and start making changes in their own life.

Thanks so much!
Laurie

My Gift To You

I am so grateful that you're here!

As my Gift to you, get FREE Access to the accompanying Audiobook by scanning the QR Code below or visiting

www.artsforlifeproductions.com

www.ingramcontent.com/pod-product-compliance
Lightning Source LLC
Chambersburg PA
CBHW061732120626
46550CB00005B/1778